MARGUERITE DURAS

MARGUERITE DURAS

Fascinating Vision and Narrative Cure

Deborah N. Glassman

Rutherford ● Madison ● Teaneck
Fairleigh Dickinson University Press
London and Toronto: Associated University Presses

Associated University Presses
440 Forsgate Drive
Cranbury, NJ 08512

Associated University Presses
25 Sicilian Avenue
London WC1A 2QH, England

Associated University Presses
P.O. Box 39, Clarkson Pstl. Stn.
Mississauga, Ontario,
L5J 3X9 Canada

The paper used in this publication meets the requirements of the American National Standard for Permanence of Paper for Printed Library Materials Z39.48-1984.

Library of Congress Cataloging-in-Publication Data

Glassman, Deborah N., 1950–
    Marguerite Duras : fascinating vision and narrative cure / Deborah N. Glassman.
        p.   cm.
    Includes bibliographical references and index.
    ISBN 0-8386-3337-4 (alk. paper)
    1. Duras, Marguerite—Criticism and interpretation.   I. Title.
PQ2607.U8245Z68   1991
843'.912—dc20   88-46147
                                                                      CIP

PRINTED IN THE UNITED STATES OF AMERICA

Contents

MARGUERITE DURAS

1

Presenting Marguerite Duras

In 1984, Marguerite Duras was awarded France's most prestigious literary award, the Goncourt Prize for *L'Amant*. The award was a double scandal. Some critics protested the committee's decision to deprive younger talent of needed and deserved support. (The Goncourt is worth only about fifty francs in cash but dramatically affects book sales.) Others felt that official recognition of Duras's oeuvre was long overdue,[1] and that this mostly first-person autobiography offered long-awaited revelations.[2]

Duras began publishing novels toward the end of the Second World War, although some of her more journalistic manuscripts from that period did not come to light until recently, (e.g., *La Douleur*). Duras's first novel, *Les Impudents,* appeared in 1943 and was followed by *La Vie tranquille* in 1944. Six years later, she published *Un Barrage contre le Pacifique,* the first of many novels subsequently adapted for the stage and/or used as the basis for later films.[3] Literary historians situate her among the generation of French postwar writers influenced by Faulkner and Hemingway,[4] but many have difficulty categorizing her work.

In the fifties, when an active polemic was carried on among readers, writers, and critics of the new writing practices, but before the "New Novelists" were baptized as such or anthologized, Duras was considered one of the talented young writers of her generation.[5] In a special issue of *Esprit* featuring a selection of popular and visible novelists, she was included on the list of ten "romanciers plus ou moins fréquemment cités à propos de ce que les critiques très divers . . . ont appelé . . . la nouvelle école du roman . . . nouveau réalisme . . . l'anti-roman" (novelists more or less frequently quoted regarding what very different critics . . . have called . . . the new school of the novel . . . new realism . . . antinovel).[6] This list might be considered a contemporary index of literary tastes as well as a chronicle of the critical reception of the emerging "school." Duras was one of only two women cited; Nathalie Sarraute was the other.[7] Indeed, the mobility of the narrative eye in Duras's texts, as well as the presentation of a number of parallel interpretations, justifies her place within the Ecole du Regard (a term that best describes the wing dominated by Robbe-Grillet).[8]

Some critics felt that Duras had disappointed her early promise. "[I]n the light of her subsequent works [after 1952] one can readily appreciate how much promise she showed and potential originality she already possessed. The turning point came in 1953. . . . As soon as Marguerite Duras decided to establish herself opposite, beside or on the frontier of, the 'abstract novel,' things began to go a bit wrong."[9] When the New Novel was studied in the seventies and early eighties, Duras's name was mentioned as often as not. She was difficult for some critics to take seriously.[10] Many had difficulty appreciating "l'économie des mots, [et] la minceur de l'intrigue [qui] rapprochent ce récit d'un poème" (the sparseness of her language, [and] the thinness of her plots [which] make her tales resemble poems).[11] The novels of the late forties and fifties were then, and continue to be, stylistically tame. From the late fifties onward, Duras becomes more of a minimalist, paring her sentences and her vocabulary, as well as her tales, down to a spareness that may or may not be taken as essentialism, but which, in all cases, increases the force of each word. Duras was not long for the canonized ranks and slipped from a position of prominence to a rather more marginal one. But she was not entirely correct in saying that "les gens comprennent mal ce que je fais" (people don't understand what I am doing) and suffered from the "silence général sur moi" (general silence about me),[12] for her marginalization was never absolute.

The critical silence or misunderstanding that surrounded Duras's work until relatively recently, doubtless stems from a number of factors. Her style and virtuosity, along with the polymorphous nature of her texts and their intricate intertextuality, frustrate the academic classifying impulse. Her style of the last twenty years is so distinct that it has been parodied in print.[13] Duras is a tale-teller in the oral tradition, one who repeats and amplifies a story as she tells it in her minimal vocabulary, drawing her listeners in. Her rhythms are occasionally pulmonary; run-on sentences rush forward only to stop, y. More typically, her sentences are short and exhibit her and remarkable taste for repetition. Words, entire passages, are repeated as if she were testing her choices, digesting the shape of her ideas or of the adjectives with which she modifies her nouns, changing them *andando*. (Or, more rhetorically put, *amplificando*.) Dominique Noguez, one of Duras's primary critical interpreters, offers an excellent analysis of her style, beginning with Duras's use of parataxis and repetition. Duras juxtaposes rather than subordinates her short sentences. This predilection for parataxis has the effect of slowing her tale down, of reducing the forward momentum of her narrative in favor of a temporal expansion. Like certain of her repetitions which, Noguez argues, "[O]nt pour but de dilater le temps de la lecture, comme pour le faire coïncider avec la durée supposée de ce qui est décrit" (take as their goal the dilation of reading time as if to make it coincide with the time of the fiction).[14] Duras's use of parataxis and repetition are thus "la marque d'une lente conquête sur l'incertain" (the sign of a slow conquest over uncertainty).[15] Uncertainty would be conquered, then, slowly, in the discovery and addition of, say, an adjective. But another and perhaps the most often remarked type of repetition in Duras's writing is the emphatic use of a pronoun or proper noun. Abundant use of the emphatic does not diminish her equally characteristic use of synecdochical pariphrase for a proper name. Thus, "son nom be Venise" for Anna Maria Guardi. These two stylistic devices would seem to serve different purposes; precision in the first and generalization in the second. Duras's use of proper names (and of singular paraphrases or antinomases), claims Noguez, is almost metaphysical. Names are proffered in the equivalent of hushed tones. An attenuated form of silence.

Often proclaiming the insufficiencies of language, Duras demonstrates the insufficiencies of narrative categories to define the nature of her tales. The temporal dimensions of her texts are difficult to define because her tense of predilection, the past conditional, situates her plots somewhere—but where?—between fiction, hallucination, fantasy, and memory. The experiments of the New Novelists, attempting as they did to forge a new postwar subjectivity, now seem tame. Duras's style, however, poetic in its density and terseness, however musical in its form, continues to aggravate and mesmerize her readers.

Duras is probably at her best in novels and films. While she writes in a number of genres, which makes her difficult to pigeonhole, she does so with unequal success. Her stageplays present psychologically dramatic situations that often seem wooden on stage. The dramas do not unfold and there is little development onstage, for everything has usually already happened. Her novels and films are lately better appreciated, due partly to their formal daring. The interest of these novels and films notwithstanding, their intertextuality is complex. A novel may be published, followed by a film that is not an adaptation of the novel—but what is it? A single text might appear as a play or as a novel, and the sound track of a film may be used as the sound track for another film, creating confusing relationships between the texts.[16] Duras is difficult to categorize; she is more difficult to dismiss.

Duras's pulsing stories produce powerful effects on her readers. If for some she is boring, for others she is fascinating. "A partir de *Lol V. Stein. . . . [sic]* Je sais que quand je lis vos livres, ça me met dans un état très . . . très fort et je suis très mal à l'aise et c'est très difficile de parler ou de faire quelque chose, après les avoir lus . . . c'est vraiment un état dans lequel il est dangereux d'entrer."[17] (Starting with *Lol V. Stein. . . . [sic]* I know that when I read your books, they put me in a very, very powerful state and I am ill at ease and it is difficult to talk or to do anything after having read them. It is really a state into which it is dangerous to enter.) The merits of Duras's work are not evident to all, but all have strong reactions to her.[18]

Rather than arguing for or against any one of the critical opinions about Duras, we might begin by considering the relative thematic unity of her oeuvre. Its range is restricted and as traditional as Stendhal, Balzac, and Flaubert. She tells tales of adulterous love and murderous family passions in which her heroines, who interest her more than do the male characters, are often stifled by their bourgeois universe.[19] If the range of Duras's themes is limited, however, she makes up in intensity for what she lacks in variety. Her texts chart landscapes of loss in which compassless characters are unable either fully to forget the past or embrace the present. Characteristically, it is her female characters who are absorbed in mourning their pasts, and particularly their past love affairs. They seek the sanctuary of memory in order to preserve the intensity of their experience from the erosion of time. If memory succeeds in preserving their experience, however, the universe of memories can become more compelling than that of ongoing time. Duras's heroines are therefore often absorbed and absent. Duras is fascinated by stories about absorption; she is fascinated by her characters' fascination with their own fictions.

s's themes are consonant with those of more traditional nov-
treatment of them is not. The importance of the temporality

and invention of memory, the manner in which characters obsessively turn around past events, and the close attention accorded sexual passions, place Duras's work within a discourse accessible to the logic of psychoanalysis.[20] Drawing on a psychoanalytic vocabulary to describe this oeuvre is justified by the romanesque universe of Duras's characters, the nature of her themes, and the manner in which the themes inform the structure of the texts. Additionally, this vocabulary is in some sense confirmed by Duras's own invocation of it in the course of rather long interviews and discussions of her work. She describes the memory of an early event as a "primal scene,"[21] and speaks about the circulation of desire among the characters in her novels, invoking terms familiar to readers of Lacan. It is likely that Duras employs these terms in a loose rather than a clinical way, for this is a vocabulary that has common coin and is casually invoked in literary circles, among others. But insofar as Duras does have recourse to a vocabulary that springs from a conceptual universe which Freud and his disciples elaborated, and that is broadly useful to approach the thematic preoccupations and formal design of her work, we offer a psychoanalytic framework as an appropriate and useful one with which to read her work. This is by no means to claim that Duras's work is an argument for Freudian orthodoxies. It is not. The Freudian dispensation will not be invoked here as a model for reading Duras, but rather as a point of reference that her work, in its turn, implicitly questions.[22]

One of the great problems confronting Freud as he undertook to write his patients' case histories, was the orchestration of the different moments of the story he was telling.[23] There was the patient's history—that of the neurosis—and the history of the patient's slow recall of his or her past, and that of Freud's reworking of those memories into a case history. The operation of the unconscious upon memory and its impact on telling tales and writing narratives is one of Freud's great themes. It is also a central theme in Duras's work where her male narrators demonstrate an unwavering faith in the restorative powers of language. For the Durasian heroine, however, the domestication of memory in language dilutes the intensity of the lived event. Duras's ravishing and ravished heroines are suspended in the timelessness of their memories and emotions. They defy the male narrators who would exorcize their fascination with the past ⌐ their stories.

Bent on rewriting heroines back into time with a na⌐

history, Duras's narrators resemble archaeologists piecing together fragments to produce a whole object or complete picture of the past. Frequently, these narrators are chronicler-healers. They make stories to liberate their "patients" from their pasts. This universe of traumatized heroines attended to by self-appointed tale-tellers, suggests a therapeutic setting in which the parallel between patients and heroines and analysts and narrators is gender-specific. The analysts-narrators are male, while the hysterical and unwilling patients are female. The analogy between a fictional universe and a therapeutic one raises a question about the limits of narrative. Can telling stories cure?

Not all stories can be told. Some stories elude narrative frames.[24] In a discussion about the length and efficacy of psychoanalytic therapy, Freud observed that analysis has its limits, differentiating between curable and incurable or recurrent neuroses.[25] He took a cautious stance on the widespread applicability of the "talking cure." Duras's heroines are more than cautious; they resist the equation between narrative and cure, choosing instead to inhabit the universe of their memories. If Duras's heroines attest to Freud's belief that talking may provide a release from the symptoms of unconscious and apparently unremembered events and desires, they do so only negatively.

It is not surprising that psychoanalysts and critics interested in psychoanalysis are among Duras's partisans. For despite the general silence from which she says she has suffered, Duras has had a faithful audience in France and in the States since as far back as the sixties and seventies. For if she was a marginal figure, as she claimed, she was a marginal cult figure. In France, her novels and films were read and lauded by feminist critics and others who had a common interest in exploring the psychosexual and social constructions of the subject. If they came from different critical domains, these critics nonetheless shared an interest in the relationship between the subject and the semiotic systems shaping and splitting it—the family, gender, and language. Although they lauded Duras, these critics tend to see in her an exemplary Woman Writer, one who either writes by somehow directly transcribing her soul, her silence, and her madness, or one who demonstrates, with her spare novels, the absence that marks a woman's place in a phallocentric world.[26] Similarly, Duras's partisans on this side of the Atlantic were few and specialized, Francophiles primarily, feminists, specialists of French literature and cinéphiles. In 1959, her screenplay for *Hiroshima mon amour* became one of the stunning successes of the French New Wave and remains a mainstay of film courses and international film festivals. In 1976, when *India Song* played at the Little Carnegie in New York City, Duras's intellectual brand of movie-making was applauded.[27]

The Goncourt, then, did not make an unknown writer famous, but it did significantly broaden Duras's audience. Since receiving it she has attained a previously unknown international prominence. The award was not only, as some believed, a corrective to the committee's earlier exclusion of Duras, but it also confirmed the longer-standing shift in the critical center of gravity. Critics taking avant-garde positions had already found Duras compelling in the late sixties and early seventies; they have since become more powerful voices in academic critical debates. Since the midseventies and early eighties, Lacanian psychoanalysis, feminist theory, and semiotic film theory have moved into the center of academic discourse and even come to popular attention. The silence of which Duras complained was broken in some measure by this redefinition of a critical center and by the attendant scrutiny of the traditional literary canons.[28] Appreciation for her work has grown as a result of her own evolution, as well.

Love stories and concern with sexual passion have always dominated Duras's oeuvre, but from the late fifties on, her style and formal concerns have crystallized. Toward the end of the decade, Duras began to focus increasingly on very specific themes. *Moderato cantabile*, published in 1958, marked a change in her writing practice and in her social relationships.[29] In that novel, she describes a heroine who refuses a bourgeois universe and seeks her own rhetorical destruction with the help of a proletarian tale-teller. Similarly, the female protagonist of the 1959 screenplay for *Hiroshima mon amour* revolts against the protocol of her bourgeois world, during a period of madness and willful suspension of time.[30] This novel and film herald Duras's intense exploration of the relationship between trauma, memory, visual experience, and narration.

Taken together, *Moderato cantabile* and *Hiroshima mon amour* constitute a turning point in Duras's work. Examining them, we will see Duras's formal strategies and thematic concerns emerge. This examination will provide the background for a longer, more in-depth discussion of two of the most important texts in which her focus on trauma, memory, and narration is the most sustained and intense, *Le Ravissement de Lol V. Stein* and *India Song*, the inaugural novel and penultimate film of the Indian Cycle.[31] If the structure of the Indian

Cycle is not cyclical in the medieval sense of a coherent group of works with a progressive chronology, the three novels and three films written and directed by Duras between 1964 and 1976, share a cast of characters, settings, and chronology whose absent origin is the unassimilable trauma of the eponymous heroine of *Le Ravissement de Lol V. Stein*.[32] *India Song*, released a dozen years after *Le Ravissement de Lol V. Stein*, is the most powerful film in the group.[33] Finally, we will look at the autobiographical *L'Amant* in the context of a discussion of Duras's biography, together with an earlier autobiographical novel, *Un Barrage contre le Pacifique*. These discussions will allow us to observe the process by which Duras's oeuvre is constituted.

The organizing principle of the discussion is to pair texts, generally a novel and a film. This selection does not imply that the films are adaptations of the novels; Duras's exploration of the limits of language and her thematic obsession with memory, whose logic and force is one of her primary preoccupations and for which she often uses the metaphor of the cinema, lead her to a visual medium. Moreover, visual fascination and fantasy, central themes in her novels, are integral to the structure of the cinema. Cinema, with its twin axes of identification and fascination, is the natural medium in which Duras can move beyond the limits of narrative.[34] The two texts from the *Indian Cycle*, together with the two autobiographical novels provide a general mapping of the circulation of formal concerns and thematic obsessions set in place in *Moderato cantabile* and in *Hiroshima mon amour*.

Duras is a prolific and provocative writer whose work cannot be confined to a single school or genre. No single study of her work can be definitive. This choice of texts and invocation of a psychoanalytic framework from which to consider them, are made in the hope of providing some useful tools for approaching the Durasian imagination.[35]

Transitional Works and the Real Writing:
Moderato cantabile and *Hiroshima mon amour*

Moderato cantabile[36] is a frontier text, for with it Duras repudiates her prior work. "Il y a toute une période où j'ai écrit des livres, jusqu'à *Moderato cantabile*, que je ne reconnais pas." (There is an entire period when I wrote books, up until *Moderato cantabile*, that I do not recognize.)[37] The novel does not introduce radically new themes; family dramas of frustrated maternal passion and traumatized sensibilities are at the heart of the earlier *Un Barrage contre le Pacifique*. There, the ties between mothers and children are equally complicated and unspoken. What is new in *Moderato cantabile* is the narrative form. Duras's dazzlingly fractured narrative is filled with abruptly shifting descriptions that move the reader from interior to exterior, for example, with little warning or apparent justification. The highly formal, anonymous narrating consciousness establishes visual analogies between spaces whose boundaries are unclear. Similarly, the temporal demarcations of the action, such as it is, are ambiguous. Despite such indications of a traditionally linear chronology—"they met on the third day," for example,—the plot moves forward as a recapitulation. Something has already taken place. Repetition, rather than development, characterizes the narrative structure. The novel's title offers a key to its organization, which is musical rather than discursive.

With *Moderato cantabile*, Duras breaks with her early, more traditional writing. The characteristics that emerge here herald an enduring writing style and set of preoccupations: the curious and enthralling relationship between a spectacular display of traumatic passion, memory, and representation, and the exploration of the limits of those relationships. Language, memory, and fantasy cohabit uneasily here in this first of Duras's "sincere" texts.

Moderato cantabile

Une expérience érotique très, très, très violente. . . . [J]'ai traversé une crise qui était . . . suicidaire, c'est à dire que ce que je raconte dans *Moderato cantabile*, cette femme qui veut être tuée, je l'ai vécu . . . et à partir de là, les livres ont changé. . . . J'ai pensé à ça depuis deux ans, deux, trois ans, je pense que le tournant, le virage vers la sincérité s'est produit là. Et, comme dans *Moderato cantabile*, la personnalité de l'homme avec qui je vivais ne comptait pas. Enfin, ce n'était pas une histoire . . . d'amour, mais une histoire . . . sexuelle. [J]e l'ai racontée de l'extérieur dans *Moderato cantabile*. . . .[38]

A very, very, very violent erotic experience. I went through a crisis which was . . . suicidal, which is to say that what I talk about in *Moderato cantabile*, this woman who wants to be killed, I lived it . . . and from that moment on, my books changed. I have thought about it for the last two years, two, three years, I think that the turning point, the turn towards sincerity came at that moment. And, like in the novel, *Moderato cantabile,* the personality of the man with whom I was living did not count. Well it was not a . . . love story, but a . . . sexual story. I have spoken of it obliquely in *Moderato cantabile.* . . .

MUSICAL TIME

Moderato cantabile explores the limits of, and relationship between, passion, visual fascination, and narration. It is a tale of passion and inebriation, of a woman's passion for her child, of her fascination with a love crime, and of her slow disaffection from her bourgeois life. The title of the novel gives an indication of its tempo and mood. Told in a series of eight brief chapters that build slowly to internal points of climax while recapitulating the unseen passional crime, the novel unfolds in an ambiguous narrative region somewhere between fantasy and memory. Disorientating, *Moderato cantabile* was, for conservative critics, the point at which Duras went wrong.

Anne Desbaresdes is a bourgeois housewife with little to do. She loves her son with boundless passion.[39] Her other affective ties go largely unremarked. Weekly, she attends piano lessons in his teacher's apartment. The teacher is frustrated. Music is not important to the recalcitrant boy who is inattentive to the score. When he reads "Moderato cantabile," he sullenly claims not to understand how to interpret the instructions, despite many explanations. The teacher blames Anne's indulgence for her child's behavior. Anne suffers through the lesson silently, unable to be angry with this son.

We are in a universe of sounds that are the language of emotion narrated by an unnamed narrator who focuses on Anne. Her voice, more important than any other sound for her son, assures the child of her existence. Sounds permeate the apartment where the music lesson lurches forward. Those of the small seaport in which the novel is set, of the ocean, of boat whistles, of the soft purring of ship engines. The polyphony of random sounds creates an impression of boundarylessness in a porous universe.

Music, like narrative, is shaped by silences and repetitions that inflect a phrase or a motif. *Moderato cantabile* is shaped by repetitions; the principal of these is a scripted recapitulation of the scene that takes place at the novel's outset while two minor repetitions accompany the primary one. The characters are engaged in a storytelling that is contrapuntal, and the chapters are arranged in a spatial counterpoint of café and piano lesson; the two spaces are sutured by the sounds of the piano and the screams. The novel is musical in its architecture.

The piano lesson is disrupted by a woman's scream. Unlike the other atmospheric noises that are noted by the anonymous narrating consciousness, this one elicits comment from the characters. "Dans la rue, en bas de l'immeuble, un cri de femme retentit. Une plainte longue, continue, s'éleva et si haut que le bruit de la mer en fut brisé. Puis elle s'arrêta net. Qu'est-ce que c'est? cria l'enfant. Quelque chose est arrivé dit la dame" (13). (In the street downstairs a woman screamed, a long drawn-out scream so shrill it overwhelmed the sound of the sea. Then it stopped abruptly. What was that?" the child shouted. "Something happened," says the lady" (78).[40] Something has already taken place before Anne reaches the scene; the scream is the only moment of the crime that Anne lives first-hand. And indeed, the scream becomes a leitmotif—the novel could have been called the scream for the sirens and human cries of birth and of death, which resound and mark the time.

SPECTACULAR PASSIONS

Pushing through the crowd at the café entrance, Anne is drawn to a scene of grief. A man has just killed his lover. Her corpse is lying on the floor while the stricken murderer supplicates her to return to him, caressing her hair and kissing her bloodied mouth, indifferent to the presence of the silent crowd. When the police come, he yields to them, but then disengages himself to return furiously to the body.

The scene becomes an obsession for Anne, who changes her daily rhythms. What had been weekly trips to the piano teacher's apartment become daily pilgrimages to the café. At the scene of the crime she begins to drink. Unaware of the incongruity that her patronage and drunkenness pose in this working-class setting, Anne continues. She encounters a worker at the bar who introduces himself as Chauvin. Chauvin is an ex-employee at her husband's factory. He knows Anne. He has watched her come and go for a year. He remembers her from the receptions her husband gave for his workers. Anne does not recognize Chauvin. Both have returned ineluctably to the café. "Il m'aurait été impossible de ne pas revenir, dit-elle enfin. —Je suis revenu moi aussi pour la même raison que vous" (34). ("It would have been impossible for me not to come back," she said finally. And I came back for the same reason as you") (90). Why?

Like Anne, Chauvin is fascinated by a remembered scene, but their meetings serve primarily to co-write a scenario for the murder that has taken place at the café and that will allow Anne to detach herself from her bourgeois universe. At the same time they embark on this enterprise, each invokes another obsessional and personal tale. Anne recalls the birth of her son (a tale that also begins with a scream) and avows the passionate love she bears him while Chauvin invokes a fantasy or memory of Anne at a reception at her home held a year before. She stands, he says, before an open window. "Devant une certaine fenêtre du premier étage, dit-il. . . . Au mois de juin de l'année dernière, il y aura un an dans quelques jours, vous vous teniez face à lui sur le perron prête à nous accueillir, nous, le personnel des Fonderies. Au dessus de vos seins à moitié nus, il y avait une fleur blanche de magnolia" (57). (It would be easy to mistake that garden from a distance, since it's enclosed and overlooks the sea. [sic] Last June—in a few days it will be a year ago—you were standing facing him [sic] on the steps, ready to receive us, the workers from the foundries. Above your breasts, which were half bared, there was a white magnolia" (105). Later in the novel: "Vous étiez accoudée à ce grand piano. Entre vos seins nus sous votre robe, il y a cette fleur de magnolia" (79). ("You were leaning on the grand piano. Between your breasts, naked beneath your dress, there is this magnolia flower"). Like Anne, Chauvin is fascinated by an erotic scene, his gaze focusing on the fetishized magnolia blossom set between Anne's breasts, a scene he ceaselessly invokes, his script arranged. Remembered or imagined, it signals the desire at the heart of his narrative enterprise. Their different scripts, like so many musical voices, organize the narrative.

THE NARRATIVE ENTERPRISE

Chauvin and Anne are well suited to their communion. Each is fascinated and eager to nourish the other's obsession by telling stories. Chauvin will, in his turn, beg Anne to talk to him. "Inventez, parlez-moi, racontez." (Make it up, talk to me, tell the story.) Chauvin knows little about the couple's history. "J'ai essayé de savoir davantage. Je ne sais rien" (41). (I tried to find out something more. But I couldn't") (94). "Vous savez, je sais très peu de choses" (84). (You know, I know very little.) Anne relishes the most lurid moments of the scene by repeating the details to herself in a rapturous manner. "Du sang sur la bouche, dit-elle, et il l'embrassait, l'embrassait" (33). ("Blood on her mouth," she said, "and he was kissing her, kissing her" (89). The paroxysm of violence and passion that resolved itself in the woman's death becomes the focus of her obsession and the teleology of her encounters with Chauvin.

Vous croyez quand même que c'est elle qui a commencé à le dire, à oser le dire et qu'ensuite il en a été question entre eux comme d'autre chose. . . . Est-ce de la douleur de l'avoir tuée, qu'elle soit morte, que cet homme est devenu fou, ou autre chose s'est-il ajouté de plus loin à cette douleur, autre chose que les gens ignorent en général?" . . . (48)
Je voudrais que vous me disiez maintenant comment ils en sont arrivés à ne plus se parler. . . . (54)
Du moment qu'il avait compris qu'elle désirait tant qu'il le fasse, je voudrais que vous me disiez pourquoi il ne l'a pas fait, par exemple, un peu plus tard ou . . . un peu plus tôt. (84)

You think it was she who first brought it up, who first dared mention it, and that then they talked about it together as they talked about other things? Is it the grief of having killed her, of her being dead, that drove him mad, or something else from his past added to that grief, something no one knows? (98–99)
I'd like you to tell me how they came not to speak to each other any more. (102). . . .
Once he had realized how much she wanted him to do it, I'd like you to tell me why he didn't do it, say, a little later or . . . a little sooner. (122)

When Chauvin declares, "Mais je crois qu'il l'a visée au coeur comme elle le lui demandait" (33) ("But I think he aimed at her heart, just as she asked him to" (90), Anne's reaction is sensual; the story of the murder excites her. "Anne Desbaresdes gémit. Une plainte presque licencieuse, douce, sortit de cette femme" (33). (Anne Desbaresdes sighed. A soft, almost erotic sigh) (90). Over the course of ten days, fantasy and history become indistinguishable as Chauvin and Anne pursue their ritual dialogues.

With mounting intensity, the two characters retrace the moments of the first couple's tragedy. Anne begs Chauvin to shape the couple's story, to give it a beginning and a middle that justify the end. "—Je voudrais que vous me disiez le commencement même, comment ils ont commencé à se parler. C'est dans un café, disiez-vous . . ." (44). (I'd like you to tell me about the very beginning, how they began to talk to each other. It was in a café, you said . . . (96). Keeping her wine glass filled, Chauvin embellishes his story of the couple—an avowed fiction that bears a striking resemblance to his actual situation with Anne.

> Il lui tendit un verre de vin tout en riant. —Cette femme était devenue une ivrogne. On la trouvait le soir dans les bars de l'autre côté de l'arsenal, ivre morte. On la blâmait beaucoup. . . . (55–56)

> Oui, je crois bien que c'est dans un café qu'ils ont commencé à se parler, à moins que ce soit ailleurs. Ils ont peut-être parlé de la situation politique, des risques de guerre, ou bien d'autre chose encore de bien différent de tout ce qu'on peut imaginer, de tout, de rien. (44)

> He laughed as he handed her a glass of wine. "That woman had become a drunkard. At night people found her in the bars out beyond the dock-yards, stone drunk. There was a lot of bad talk." (104)

> "Yes, I believe that it was in a café that they began to talk, unless it was somewhere else. Maybe they talked about the political situation, or the chances of war, or maybe something totally different from anything we can imagine, about everything and nothing." (97)

The roles of raconteur and listener oscillate and shift; the counter-point is perfect. Just as Anne begged Chauvin to tell her their story, he now insists that she speak to him. "—Dites-moi encore, dit Chauvin, vous pouvez me dire n'importe quoi" (61). ("Tell me more," Chauvin said, "you can tell me anything at all" (107). To which Anne answers with anecdotes about the town, the weather, and her house. In their final encounter at the café, Chauvin and Anne embrace and finalize the mise-en-scène. With a moan, Anne announces her response to Chauvin's borrowed desire that she die; her death takes place in narrative with a typically Durasian note.

> [E]lle se mit à gémir doucement une plainte impatiente . . . perceptible qu'à lui seul. . . . Une dernière fois, supplia-t-elle, dites-moi. Chauvin hésita, les yeux toujours ailleurs . . . puis il se décida à le dire comme d'un souvenir. —Jamais auparavant, il n'aurait pensé que l'envie aurait pu lui en venir un jour. Son consentement à elle était entier? Emerveillé. Anne Desbaresdes leva vers Chauvin un regard absent. . . . Je voudrais comprendre un peu pourquoi était si merveilleuse son envie qu'il y arrive un jour. —Ce n'est pas la peine d'essayer de comprendre. On ne peut pas comprendre à ce point. . . . J'ai peur, murmura Anne Desbaresdes. J'ai peur, dit de nouveau Anne Desbaresdes. Chauvin ne répondit pas. J'ai

peur, cria presque Anne Desbaresdes. Chauvin ne répondit toujours pas.
Anne Desbaresdes se plia en deux presque jusqu'à toucher la table de son
front et elle accepta la peur. . . . Peut-être que je ne vais pas y arriver,
murmura-t-elle. . . . C'est impossible, dit-elle. Je voudrais que vous
soyez morte, dit Chauvin. C'est fait, dit Anne Desbaresdes. (109–14)

Then, in her impatience, she moaned softly—so softly that the sound of
the radio covered it, and he alone heard it. "One last time," she begged.
Chauvin hesitated, his eyes somewhere else, still fixed on the back wall.
Then he decided to tell her about it as if it were a memory. "He had never
dreamed before meeting her, that he would one day want anything so
badly." "And she acquiesced completely. . . ." "Wonderfully." "I'd like to
know why his desire to have it happen one day was so wonderful?"
"There's no use trying to understand. It's beyond understanding." "I'm
afraid," Anne Desbaresdes murmured. . . . "I'm afraid," she almost
shouted. Still Chauvin did not reply. Anne Desbaresdes doubled over, her
forehead almost touching the table, and accepted her fear. "Maybe I won't
be able to," she murmured. "That's impossible," she said. "I wish you
were dead," Chauvin said. "I am," Anne Desbaresdes said. (137–40)

Anne is not atypical of Duras's heroines, whose "deaths" are inti-
mately linked with narrative and with traumatic passion.

RITUAL VICTIMS

Chapter 7 links Anne's narrative death with that of her bourgeois
existence. The penultimate of the novel's eight short divisions describes a dinner party. Anne's alcoholism, nourished by Chauvin's
attention to her wine glass along with her indecorous disaffection
from her guests, prevent her from carrying out her duties as hostess.[41]
Not only is she late and offering no excuses to her guests or husband,
but she is also without appetite or conversation. Wearing the familiar
low-cut gown and magnolia between her breasts, Anne strikes a pose
near the grand piano. Her wardrobe may well be quite limited, but
this punctual appearance of low-cut gown and magnolia, together
with her stance near the piano cannot but recall Chauvin's earlier
memory. Who narrates this scene? What space does it occupy in the
novel? Is it part of Chauvin's fantasy? Or is Anne dressed in homage
to Chauvin? The boundaries between fiction, memory, and fantasy
are blurred and the reader is situated in a familiarly ambiguous
narrative space.

The dinner party constitutes a ritual, a polite cannibalization.
Familial silver and genteel napery drape the table, which serves as an
altar for the entrée of salmon, once a denizen "des eaux libres," and

the second course of duck, which arrives on its shroud of oranges. These are the victims that Anne's bejeweled guests consume but from whose consumption she abstains. Less and less able to participate in the feast, her loss of appetite parallels Chauvin's. He is not one of the guests, but is described as being near the beach, where, frustrated by unconsummated desires, he paces, or is imagined pacing. Outside, "un homme seul regarde tantôt la mer, tantôt le parc. Puis la mer, le parc, ses mains. Il ne mange pas. Il ne pourrait pas, lui non plus, nourrir son corps tourmenté d'autre faim. L'encens des magnolias arrive toujours sur lui" (96). ([B]eyond the white blinds lay darkness, and in this darkness a man, with plenty of time to kill, stands looking now at the sea, now at the garden. Then at the sea, at the garden, at his hands. He doesn't eat. He cannot eat either, his body obsessed by another hunger. The capricious wind still bears the scent of magnolias to him) (129). Chauvin escapes the stultifying space of the overfed.[42]

By the end of the chapter, Anne is entirely disaffected from her cohorts. She finishes the evening distended and vomiting on her son's bedroom floor, repudiating her bourgeois universe from her only affective port.[43] This purgative gesture is a prelude to her narrative death. If, however, Anne is moved by her narrative transformation, Chauvin, like many of Duras's male protagonists, remains in his ancillary role; his desire goes unsatisfied.

A year after publishing *Moderato cantabile*, Duras continues her meditation on visual fascination and narration. The process of giving a narrative form to a perceived or remembered fascinating erotic spectacle is once again at the heart of *Hiroshima mon amour*. The screenplay focuses on two different but equally unassimilable traumata, the one personal and the second historical.[44] Its surprising juxtaposition of a first-person pronoun and strongly connotative noun summarizes the challenge that Duras poses to the possibility of personal historiography as well as to History writ large. Taken together with *Moderato cantabile*, *Hiroshima mon amour* indicates a sharpening of Duras's thematic focus and a broadening of her fields of formal expression.

Hiroshima mon amour

C'est avec *Hiroshima mon amour* que le nom de Marguerite Duras a atteint le grand public. [C]e film est une excellente introduction à son oeuvre.[45]

Hiroshima mon amour is a confusing and disturbing film that received a great deal of critical praise and attention after its 1959 screening. The *Cahiers du Cinéma* adopted it as their darling and entitled its July 1959 issue, *Hiroshima notre amour*.[46] Applauded for its successful treatment of the temporality of memory and of the intrusion of the past into the present, the film was a collaborative effort between Duras, who wrote the screenplay, and Alain Resnais, who directed the visuals.[47] The partnership was fairly independent— Duras wrote the screenplay before the film was shot—and successful because of the partners' shared interest in the play of memory and in politics.[48]

Duras's interest in the relationship between memory as visual experience, and its representation in language, is every bit as intense as Resnais's single-minded focus on time and memory.[49] Resnais has been characterized as a director nostalgic for some mythic unity and engaged in a project of cinematic reunification of a fragmented origin. His style is a response to his desire to fathom human memory; long takes and a traveling camera create an illusion of unity.[50] His acute sense of editing lends cohesion to the images.[51]

Beyond the compatibility of their thematic concerns, Duras and Resnais can be taken as examples of French postwar artistic movements. The New Novel and the New Wave Cinema shared a common enterprise of breaking with prewar esthetic traditions as a response to postwar sensibilities. "Le roman tend aujourd'hui lentement à se débarrasser de l'intrigue psychologique. Le film [*Hiroshima mon amour*] d'Alain Resnais se trouve entièrement lié à cette modification des structures romanesques. La raison en est simple. Il n'y a pas d'action, mais une sorte de double tentative pour comprendre ce que signifie une histoire d'amour."[52] (The novel today is slowly shedding psychological intrigue [plot]. Alain Renais's film is profoundly connected to this change in novelistic structures for one simple reason. There is no action, but rather a double effort to understand what a love story means.) Stylistic responses to this imperative of new definitions varied. The arts were to break with outmoded conventions but the rupture was not always appreciated by the public.

Hiroshima represented a new hybrid genre of cinema, appreciated by some for its innovations but condemned by others. "*Hiroshima* contains remarkable innovations, and reveals the possibility of a new literary cinema which could incorporate elaborate written texts and yet remain wholly cinematic. Sound, instead of explaining and supporting the visual story, is conceived as a vital and independent component."[53] The disjunction between image and voice is disorienting for the spectator accustomed to locating sound sources. Here, however, the spectator sees neither where nor from whom the sounds come.

The relationship between sound and image has almost as long a history as does the cinema itself. In the late 1920s when technology permitted the possibility of sound being incorporated into the film, some perceived it as a distraction from, and a threat to, the hegemony of the visual image. This old debate about the question of the primacy of the image continues. Film critics even today mistrust a literary cinema, claiming that where the emphasis is on language and not on the image, it is misguided. Sadoul, for example, disparaged Duras's screenplay as too literary.[54] But what does too literary mean? Duras's screenplay forces the spectator to consider the relationship of memory, trauma, and narration in terms of sound and image. Duras raises another familiar issue of the adequacy of word to image or image to language. Hers is the question of the adequacy of narration to memory. At its heart, Duras's meditation closely parallels Resnais's own view of the cinema as a restorative enterprise. If Resnais wants to restore some primary unity to the world, Duras wants to preserve the world from the memory of rupture and subsequent loss. Together, they explore the limits of film and language as media of representation.

Hiroshima is proclaimed as a technically innovative and insightful film. The title, however, which is a program for reading the film, has been too little commented upon. We can parse it as Hiroshima *et* mon amour, Hiroshima *est* mon amour, Hiroshima *ou* mon amour or Hiroshima, mon amour! What is the link? Hiroshima is an overdetermined proper noun that evokes, for many, the atomic bombing of the Japanese city of that name. What could link such an event and a first-person love story?

The heroine, who remains anonymous throughout the film, is designated in the screenplay as Elle. Elle is a French actress who has come to Hiroshima to work on an international peace film in which she plays the role of a nurse. Toward the end of her stay in Hiroshima she meets a Japanese architect (Lui). Happily, Lui speaks French and his wife is temporarily absent from the city. They have a brief liaison which recalls Elle's painful wartime memories of her first love affair. In occupied Nevers, she meets and falls in love with a German soldier.

On the day of their planned departure for Bavaria, he is ambushed.
Elle stays with him through the night, until he dies. His body is
carted away and Nevers is liberated the following day. She is publicly
ostracized because of her liaison with an enemy soldier; her hair is
shorn to make evident her disgrace. Her parents' pharmacy is closed
because of her dishonor. The parents hide her in their cellar in order
to pass her off as dead, and in the cellar she goes mad with grief.
When she recovers, she goes to Paris. On the day she arrives, the
news of Hiroshima is everywhere. Elle subsequently marries and has
a family. Her wartime story has remained untold.

HISTORIOGRAPHY

Elle instructs us about the parallels between love and Hiroshima;
this is a lesson on reading the title. "De même que dans l'amour cette
illusion existe, cette illusion de pouvoir ne jamais oublier, de même
j'ai eu l'illusion devant Hiroshima que jamais je n'oublierai. De même
que dans l'amour" (28). (Just as in love this illusion exists, this illusion
of being able never to forget, so too, I had the illusion while confronting Hiroshima that I would never forget. Just as in love.) The analogy
that brings together two very different events is the illusion that they
are unforgettable. If unforgettability is the illusion, then forgettable is
what both Hiroshima and mon amour are. Is this analogy between a
personal trauma and an historical one justified? Hiroshima is willfully
remembered in a number of media—photographs, newsreels, museum exhibits, personal accounts, fictions, and histories. Elle's en-
gagement with her own memory is involuntary. "Nevers, tu vois,
c'est la ville du monde, et même c'est la chose du monde à laquelle, la
nuit, je rêve le plus. En même temps que c'est la chose du monde je
pense le moins" (58). (Nevers, you see, is the city in the world, and
even the thing in the world about which, at night, I dream the most.
At the same time as it is the thing in the world about which I think the
least.) Her representation is a reluctant and regretful one. What does
remembering Hiroshima mean, and how does it raise the question of
the limits of representation? Is historiography akin to the operation of
individual memory?

The gray and grainy flashback sequences are accompanied only by
music and are visually and aurally distinguishable from sequences that
constitute the film's present tense. The first of Elle's flashbacks is

extremely fleeting. After the camera pans a group of bicyclists, following Elle's line of vision from her balcony, she turns to the bedroom. There, Lui is still asleep. His hand twitches. The next shot is of another twitching hand. A wounded soldier is lying on his back. We understand that this is Elle's recollection, an involuntary flashback provoked by the visual equation between the twitching hands. Has Elle chosen a lover whose nationality sets him against France? For like the Germans, the Japanese were identified as enemies of the Allies. The war will be the focus of Lui's interest in Elle's past.

The flashback over, the action resumes in the present with Lui's request to see Elle once more. She refuses; they leave the hotel, she gets into a taxi and leaves him in a trail of dust. He later finds her on the film set from which they go to his apartment. There, Lui insists that she tell him about her past and when Elle challenges him to explain why he asks about Nevers he answers:

> A cause de Nevers, je peux seulement commencer à te connaître. Et, entre les milliers et les milliers de choses de ta vie, je choisis Nevers. C'est là il me semble avoir compris que tu es si jeune . . . si jeune que tu n'es encore à personne précisément. Cela me plaît. C'est là il me semble avoir compris que j'ai failli te perdre . . . et que j'ai risqué ne jamais te connaître. C'est là, il me semble l'avoir compris, que tu as dû commencer à être comme aujourd'hui tu es encore. (80–81)

> Because of Nevers I can only begin to know you. And among the thousands and thousands of things in your life, I choose Nevers. It is there, I seem to have understood, that you were so young . . . so young that you do not yet belong to anyone exactly. I like that. It is there, I seem to have understood, that I almost lost you . . . and that I risked never knowing you. It is there, I seem to have understood, that you began to be as you are still today.

Aided by Elle's allusions to wartime, Lui suggests that by knowing about her past, he will begin to know and, more important, possess her. He implies that the wartime trauma was formative and that from that point onward, her personality was determined. And in order to know her, he must know about her past, her traumatic past, which he cannily pinpoints. Elle balks. For if Nevers is the thing about which she dreams the most, it is the thing about which she thinks the least. She speaks about her past, her love affair, and her passion as the spectator is once again treated to the lyrical grainy flashbacks and catchy music. When later in a café, Elle begins to tell her story again and the spectator again sees grainy flashbacks, the rapid montage shows Elle and her lover meeting in the woods, making love in huts, biking through the countryside, running toward each other with outstretched arms. The music is lively and sweet, a poignant counterpoint to the tragic finale.

On devait se retrouver à midi sur le quai de la Loire. Je devais repartir avec lui. Quand je suis arrivée à midi sur le quai de la Loire il n'était pas tout à fait mort. Quelqu'un avait tiré d'un jardin. Je suis restée près de son corps toute la journée et toute la nuit suivante. Le lendemain matin on est venu le ramasser et on l'a mis dans un camion. C'est dans cette nuit-là que Nevers a été libéré. Les cloches . . . sonnaient, sonnaient. Il est devenu froid peu à peu sous moi. Ah! qu'est-ce qu'il a été long à mourir. Quand? Je ne sais plus au juste. J'étais couchée sur lui . . . oui . . . le moment de sa mort m'a échappé vraiment puisque . . . puisque même à ce-moment-là et même après, oui, même après, je peux dire que je n'arrivais pas à trouver la moindre différence entre ce corps mort et le mien. Je ne pouvais trouver entre ce corps et le mien que des ressemblances . . . hurlantes, tu comprends? C'était mon premier amour. . . . (crié) (99–100)

We were to meet at noon on the quay of the Loire. I was to leave with him. When I arrived at noon on the quay of the Loire he was not yet completely dead. Someone had shot him from a garden. It was during that night that Nevers was liberated. The church bells were ringing, ringing. Slowly he grew cold beneath me. Ah, how slowly he died! When? I don't know precisely. I was laying on him, yes, the moment of his death escaped me because . . . because even at the moment, and even afterward, yes, even afterward, I can say that I could not find the least difference between this dead body and mine. I could only find similarities between this body and mine, screaming similarities. Do you understand? It was my first love. (shouted).

When her lover was shot, Elle did not want to remember him. To the contrary, she wanted to forget that he had died. To keep the knowledge of his death at bay and to banish memory, she identified with her lover as if, through her own body's life, his could be preserved; her body becomes their common body. In this first moment, Elle becomes a metaphorical text; her body speaks the story that she will not narrate. For she stops speaking; to speak is to acknowledge the difference between herself and her lover and to admit that he has been supplanted by a word. Language is insufficient to speak the "ressemblances hurlantes." This is her madness.

Elle continues to recount her story in a trancelike state aided by the beer she gulps.[55] She addresses her dead lover; Lui responds in his voice. When she says "you," Lui answers; when Lui asks her about the cellar and about what she felt about him, her dead lover, she answers in an incantatory tone.

Je pense à toi. Je suis folle d'amour pour toi. Mes cheveux repoussent à ma main, chaque jour, je le sens. Ça m'est égal. Je ne sens rien. Tu es mort. Je suis bien trop occupée à souffrir. Ah! quelle douleur. Quelle douleur au coeur. C'est fou. On chante *La Marseillaise* dans toute la ville. Le jour tombe. Mon amour mort est un ennemi de la France.
[Lui] Et puis, un jour, mon amour, tu sors de l'éternité?
Oui, c'est long. On m'a dit que ç'avait été très long. A six heures du soir, la cathédrale Saint-Etienne sonne, été comme hiver. Un jour, il est vrai, je l'entends. Je me souviens l'avoir entendue avant—avant—pendant que nous nous aimions, pendant notre bonheur. Je commence à voir. Je me souviens avoir déjà vu—avant—avant—pendant que nous nous aimions, pendant notre bonheur. Je me souviens. Je vois l'encre. Je vois le jour. Je vois ma vie. Ta mort. Ma vie qui continue. Ta mort qui continue. . . . Ah! C'est horrible. Je commence à moins bien me souvenir de toi. Je commence à t'oublier. Je tremble d'avoir oublié tant d'amour. (97–99)

I think about you. I am mad with love for you. My hair is growing; every day I can feel it with my hand. But I don't care. I feel nothing. You are dead. I am too busy suffering. What suffering, it's unbelievable! What heartache! Night falls and the whole town sings the Marseillaise. My dead love is an enemy of France.
[He] And one day, you step out of eternity?
Yes. They told me that it was very, very long. The bells of the Cathedral Saint-Etienne ring at 6 p.m. in the summer and in the winter. And one day, it's true, I hear them ringing I remember having heard them before, before, when we loved each other, when we were happy. I begin to see again. And I remember having already seen before, before, when we loved each other, when we were happy. I remember. I see the ink. I see the day. I see my life. Your death. My life which continues. Your death which continues. It is horrible. I am beginning to remember you less well. I am beginning to forget you. I tremble at having forgotten so much love.

Narrating her exit from her madness, her eternity, and her reentry into time and mourning, Elle can now speak of memory and of a happy *before*. She remembers, she says, she sees. She sees that to remember is to remember that she has forgotten. To consider the episode cathartic would be to suggest that Elle completes a period of mourning. The intolerable loss, however, becomes intolerable forgetting. This first step in the telling of her story is, as she later sees, a step toward narrative betrayal.

In the film's penultimate sequence, Elle returns to her hotel. Standing before the bathroom mirror, she observes her reflection. In voice-over, her voice says that she has told their story. Speaking in a number of voices including her own, that of her dead lover, and that of a narrator for whom she is a third person Elle, she trivializes the events she has so painfully recalled. *Mon amour* becomes *un amour,* her private story becomes a generic tragedy, and the act of telling enacts a final self-dispossession and narrative death.

Elle a eu à Nevers un amour de jeunesse allemande. . . . Nous irons en Bavière mon amour, et nous nous marierons. Elle n'est jamais allée en Bavière. Que ceux qui ne sont jamais allés en Bavière osent lui parler de l'amour. Tu n'étais pas tout à fait mort. J'ai raconté notre histoire. Je t'ai trompé ce soir avec cet inconnu. J'ai raconté notre histoire. Elle était, vois-tu, racontable. Quatorze ans que je n'avais pas retrouvé . . . le goût d'un amour impossible. Depuis Nevers. Regarde comme je t'oublie. . . . Regarde comme je t'ai oublié. Regarde-moi. Un jour sans ses yeux et elle en meurt. Petite fille de Nevers. Petite coureuse de Nevers. Un jour sans ses mains et elle croit au malheur d'aimer. Petite fille de rien. Morte d'amour à Nevers. Petite tondue de Nevers je te donne à l'oubli ce soir. Histoire de quatre sous. Comme pour lui, l'oubli commencera par tes yeux. Pareil. Puis, comme pour lui, l'oubli gagnera ta voix. Pareil. Puis comme pour lui, il triomphera de toi tout entier, peu à peu. Tu deviendras une chanson. (110–19)

In Nevers she had a youthful love, a German. We will go to Bavaria, my love, and we will be married. She never went to Bavaria. Let those who have never gone to Bavaria dare to speak to her of love! You were not completely dead. I told our story. I deceived you tonight with this stranger. I told our story, you see, it could be told. Fourteen years have passed since I've tasted such an impossible love. Since Nevers. Look at how I am forgetting you! Look at how I have forgotten you! Look at me! A single day without his eyes and she dies. Little girl from Nevers. Little flirt from Nevers. A single day without his hands and she believes that love is torture. Worthless little girl. Dead from love in Nevers. Little shaven-headed girl from Nevers, I give you over to oblivion this night. Cheap melodrama. Just like for him, oblivion will start with your eyes. Just like for him. Then, just like for him, your voice will be forgotten. Just like for him. Then, just like him, you will be completely forgotten, little by little. You will become a song.

If the voices in which she tells her story are polyphonic, their judgment on her is univocal. Elle is guilty for telling their story just as she was once judged guilty for living it. Telling is an infidelity for it places the seal of death on the events, on the emotions, and on memory itself. Thus, while in a traditional analytic framework, telling is cathartic, here, telling the story in a coherent narrative form constitutes as much a positive catharsis as a loss. Ambiguous purgation. Elle's eulogy for her dead German lover and for her memory of him turns unflattering when she casts off the younger self who tried to preserve the illusion of unforgettable love. That girl is now banished and buried just as the citizens of Nevers judged and sentenced her long ago, she is now rhetorically dead just as her parents proclaimed her; her personal tragedy is debased. Her tale is now no more than a cheap melodrama; the translation of memory into narrative defiles even as it frees Elle.

If for Elle, making a story betrays the events it ostensibly represents, what of history writing? This question is indirectly posed from the beginning of the film that opens on two nude torsos. Depending on the filter through which they are seen, they shimmer or appear sandy. Ambiguous as much because the bodies are cropped as because there is no aural support for them, the opening shots neither reduce voices to narration nor images to illustration, a technique that will become Duras's hallmark. The voice-over dialogue debates what has been seen in Hiroshima. "J'ai tout vu à Hiroshima," says the female voice. "Tu n'as rien vu à Hiroshima," retorts the male voice. She may have gone to the museum, she may have seen the hospital wards, but she has not seen Hiroshima. There is nothing to see that tells the story of Hiroshima. Their disagreement raises many questions, including the sexual dynamics of the dispute. The Durasian heroine typically affirms the power of images to preserve events and disparages the power of language to do so.

The torso images are interrupted by long traveling shots through the city, through hospital wards, and through the Hiroshima Museum. In the museum, the atomic bombing is "explained" with the help of myriad exhibits ranging from filmed representations of burning and dying Japanese to display cases containing labeled bits of detached human hair, a melted bicycle, a stylized "explanation" of atomic power replete with lights flashing in time to jazzy music, grainy newsreel footage of the immediate aftermath of the bomb. These things are true, Elle claims; she does not invent them. For corroboration, she points to the other tourists's reactions.

—Les gens se promènent, pensifs, à travers les photographies, les reconstitutions, faute d'autre chose, à travers les photographies, les photographies, les reconstitutions, faute d'autre chose, les explications, faute d'autre chose. L'illusion, c'est bien simple, est tellement parfaite que les touristes pleurent. . . . J'ai vu les actualités. Le deuxième jour, dit l'Histoire, je ne l'ai pas inventé. . . . Je les ai vus. J'ai vu les actualités. Je les ai vues. . . .
—Tu n'as rien vu. Rien. (24, 25, 27)

People walk through the exhibits, thoughtful, through the photos, the reconstructions, for want of anything else, through the photos, the photos, the reconstruction, for want of anything else, the explanations, for want of anything else. . . . The illusion is so perfect that tourists cry. . . . I have seen the newsreels. On the second day, History tells us, I did not make it up . . . I saw them. I saw the newsreels. I saw them. You saw nothing. Nothing.

If Elle believes in visual representation, the male protagonist affirms the power of language. Their argument turns on the possibility of representation. If the trauma of Hiroshima can be equated with Elle's trauma, as one reading of the title suggests it can be, much is lost as history is written. This film takes narration to inscribe its own history as loss even as it supplants an event and its memory. Whether narrative offers a cure from the malady of obsessive memory seems ambiguous. For if it provides an exit for Elle from Nevers, she exits the poorer for the tale.

In both *Moderato cantabile* and *Hiroshima mon amour*, traumatic passion is remembered and then represented in narrative form. In each case, the trauma is in some measure linked with a woman's rejection of her bourgeois universe while its narration constitutes a male fantasy of discovery and possession. Narrative is opposed to visual memory, temporality to eternity. In each of these texts, the heroine is dispossessed of her self, at least in the narrative form which her story takes. These two relatively early texts amply document Duras's break with her more traditional writing, the emergence of a clearly musical style and what will prove to be her enduring fascination with the visual inscription of memory, fantasy, and experience. Her experimentation with, and exploration of, the limits of discursivity and the ascendancy of visual fascination in her oeuvre are dramatically demonstrated in the Indian Cycle texts, which follow.

2

Fascinating Vision and Narrative Cure:
The Ravishing of Lol V. Stein

The Indian Cycle opens with *Le Ravissement de Lol V. Stein*, a pivotal novel which Duras published in 1964.[1] Not only does *Le Ravissement de Lol V. Stein* inaugurate this unique constellation of works, but it serves as its prehistory as well. Virtually all of the subsequent Indian Cycle novels and films allude to Lol's adventure of passion and trauma. The ball at which Lol silently watches as her fiancé is enraptured, in the space of a dance, by another woman, is the mesmerizingly absent center of the Indian Cycle texts. The ball occurred ten years before the opening of *Le Ravissement*, and is mythologized in the subsequent texts whose chronologies, if ambiguous, always set the ball outside their narrative frames. In the penultimate film of the group, *India Song*, for example, the two feminine voices that we hear at the beginning, elliptically summarize Lol's story, which becomes a model for their own absorbing passion, just as it models many of the passions of these plots.

> voix 1: Michael Richardson était fiancé à une jeune fille de S. Tahla, Lola Valérie Stein. . . .
> voix 2: Le mariage devait avoir lieu à l'automne. Puis il y a eu ce bal . . . ce bal de S. Tahla.
> voix 1: Elle était arrivée tard à ce bal . . . au milieu de la nuit . . . habillée de noir
> voix 2: Que d'amour ce bal, que de désir.

> voice 1: Michael Richardson was engaged to a young girl in S. Tahla, Lola Valérie Stein.
> voice 2: The marriage was to take place in the fall. Then there was this dance, this dance in S. Tahla.
> voice 1: She had arrived late at the dance . . . in the middle of the night . . . dressed in black.
> voice 2: So much love, so much desire, this ball at S. Tahla.

During a conversation between Duras and Xavière Gauthier about the public reaction to the first of the Indian Cycle films, *La Femme du Gange* (filmed in 1972 and released confidentially in 1974),[2] Gauthier remarks that in several of what she calls Duras's frontier texts, the ball serves as a point of departure.

XG: Il y a *l'Amour, le Vice-consul, le Ravissement.* [*sic*]
MD: Et le film. Il y a trois livres et un film. . . . Brûlés, un peu. Parce que l'histoire de chacun est méprisée, sauf l'histoire du bal.
XG: L'histoire du bal, qui est toujours le point de départ.[3]

XG: There is *l'Amour, le Vice-consul, le Ravissement.* [*sic*]
MD: And the film. There are three books and a film. Burnt, a little. Because the story of each is disdained, except for the story of the ball.
XG: The story of the ball, which is always the starting point.

When Gauthier pinpoints the ball as an originary event, she does no more than corroborate the position taken by the narrator of *Le Ravissement.* According to him, the ball is a traumatogenic moment, the beginning of Lol's illness and madness. The ball thus becomes a vanishing point, the reconstructed ouverture of a fiction. It is treated as a memory, a vestige of an event that occurred well before the novel begins, a bewitching event that remains extrinsic to the narrative frames seeking to capture it; it is the starting point of numbers of Duras's texts because it consistently generates narratives and, like Lol, is never set to rest by an adequate visualization and death.[4]

Part of the magnetic attraction of the drama which occurred at the ball lies in its nature as a visual event; it is irreducible to narrative and is conserved on the lens of Lol's imagination. In attempting to reconstruct the tale of her abandonment, the narrator evokes one of the fundamental tensions in Duras's work, that between the atemporality of intense visual experience, and the will to historicize and represent that experience in narration. Broadly speaking, this is the tension between storytelling, and madness and memory delineated in *Hiroshima mon amour.* It is, moreover, characteristic not only of the internal tensions of Duras's novels, but of her oscillation between novels and films as well, in her effort to formally contain the stories that haunt her. The films, which do not transcribe her novels after which they are released as often as not, seem to set them to rest.[5] Writing thus becomes an unfinished enterprise that awaits its completion in a visual medium that offers Duras the possibility of expanding the limits of a novel, by arresting language. Indeed, Duras's production seems to come in waves. For four years after *India Song,* she stopped writing and threw herself entirely into cinematic productions. After *Le Camion,* however, she once again took up writing, and with the 1979 publication of the three poetic pieces, *Aurélia Steiner,* she was again able to give her feminine character a voice and an epistolary enterprise.

Two years after her conversation with Gauthier, Duras finished the sixth of the Indian Cycle texts. Stretter and Richardson were no longer neglected.[6] Or more correctly, Stretter was no longer neglected, for Duras's male protagonists receive far less rounding out than her female protagonists; Richardson is an ornament, rarely more than a laconic shadow. Stretter is one of the two central female protagonists of the Indian Cycle texts. No less laconic, perhaps, than Lol, she is at least as mesmerizing.

Lol and Stretter can serve to catalogue the Indian Cycle texts. The intertextuality of the histories of the Indian Cycle is complex, but the novels and films share a cast of characters that orbit around either one or the other of these two 'heroines,' Lol V. Stein or Anne-Marie Stretter. Each heroine reigns over a particular landscape. Lol deambulates in and between the municipalities typically named, of S. Tahla/T. and U. Beaches. If Lol dwells like a shadow in her natal town of S. Thala, Stretter serves a more real exile from her native Venice in Calcutta. Landscape and principal protagonists offer simple keys to the six works that can be assigned to either Lol or Stretter.

Le Ravissement de Lol V. Stein, the first and only novel of the Indian Cycle not to be released as a film, is Lol's tale.[7] When *L'Amour* (1971) revisits *Le Ravissement de Lol V. Stein* seventeen years after the ball, it does so in an "espace fantasmatique de la folie." The geographic space on which the characters promenade is T. Beach, from which they will watch S. Thala destroyed by fire.[8] These four anonymous characters—the madman, the voyager (Michael Richardson?), a madwoman (Lol Stein), and a woman in black—walk and talk on the sands.[9] *L'Amour* constitutes a stylistic end point for the novels. From its striking rhythms emerges a markedly musical and poetic text, elliptical to the point of subverting all familiar signposts of narrative. The prose no less than the characters appears dominated by fantasy pushed to madness.

La Femme du Gange, an abstract and impoverished film that evolves from *L'Amour,* is also to be catalogued with the Lol texts.[10] Shot on the windswept beach of Trouville, the static camera of this austere film focuses unblinkingly on a beach, long after the characters leave the frame. The sound track, entirely independent of the visuals, recounts Lol's story.[11] From the first novel of the Indian Cycle, the subsequent texts inherit not only the common history of the infamous ball scene, but a mounting formal tension between visual and narrative, expressed by the stationary camera and increasingly fragmented and disjunctive narratives.

The remaining three texts of the Indian Cycle are set in India and revolve around a different sun. In *Le Vice-consul* (1966), Anne-Marie Stretter is the wife of the French ambassador posted to Calcutta. Similarly, *India Song* (released in 1975) pays homage to Stretter who is virtually constantly on screen or reflected in one of the ubiquitous mirrors.[12] The film's visual obsession with Stretter is, as it were, a direct legacy of Lol; her visual fascination no less than that of Duras, is the veritable binding force of these texts. There is no mention of Lol in *Le Vice-consul*, but *India Song* clearly proclaims its ties to Lol's story. In hushed tones, the couple of female voices heard at the beginning of the film refer elliptically to her passion. *Son nom de Venise dans Calcutta désert*, the third film and final text of the cycle (1976), refers to Lol simply because its sound track is taken from *India Song*. But it is the Venetian, Stretter, whose name is shouted in deserted Calcutta. The film is shot in and around the empty Hôtel Pommereux in Paris. Its atmospherically scaling facades, windows, and statues are almost entirely purged of human presence. Identities are difficult to attribute to the occasionally visible four women seen peering from behind curtained windows. Stretter is thus present in this film in a manner similar to the way in which Lol is present in *India Song*, a memory whose distance from the visuals is incalculable and melancholic. For the spectator initiated into the universe of *India Song*, *Son nom de Venise dans Calcutta désert* is a memory twice removed, but nevertheless chronologically unsituable. When Duras projects her characters and their stories into what she calls new narrative regions, it becomes difficult to adequately describe them in terms of the old narrative categories. Familiar functions of narrator and characters, as well as the discernible entities of story and plot are poor terms with which to designate the players and contours of the Durasian universe. The provocative and elusive tale-telling of these texts may be taken as the evolution of the longer-standing aesthetic that emerges with Duras's first film.[13] Taken as a group, the novels and films of the Indian Cycle tend toward an elliptical and nondiscursive style; increasingly fascinated, less and less narrative, disseminating and reconjugating themes and images in increasingly rarefied fashion, these texts dismantle traditional literary and cinematic narrative enterprises. Clear boundaries between fiction, memory, and narration erode. Imperfect but trusted guides for describing narrative—temporal and spatial signposts—are consequently blurred. For however overused the term *fascination* may be, in the Indian Cycle texts, visual fascination is in the ascendancy.[14]

Elle est à vous, Lol V. Stein, elle est aux autres . . . et quand elle remonte vers le bal de S. Thala[15] . . . elle est déjà esquintée. . . . Ça n'a pas de sens, Lol V. Stein, voyez, ça n'a pas de signification. Lol V. Stein, c'est ce que vous en faites, ça n'existe pas autrement. . . .[16]

She belongs to you, Lol V. Stein, and she belongs to others. And when she goes back to the dance at S. Thala, she's already exhausted, faded. It does not have any meaning, you see, it does not have any significance. Lol V. Stein is what you make of her; she does not exist otherwise.

NARRATIVE CURES

Jacques Hold is the name of the narrating consciousness in this novel. In love with Lol, a peculiar, silent woman whose singularity may be attributed to an early trauma, he is attentive to her every move. When Lol was nineteen, her fiancé, Michael Richardson, abandoned her at a summer dance at T. Beach. While Lol watched, Richardson appeared to fall under the spell of a red-haired woman, a stranger who was passing through town and whose name, it was learned, was Anne-Marie Stretter. Rooted to the spot behind the potted plants of the Municipal Casino, Lol watched as the couple danced. Nor did she protest when they left the casino together. Her reaction came late, a scream and dead faint. Alerted to her daughter's state, Lol's mother arrived and brought her to the family manse where Lol spent several weeks. Did she suffer? "La prostration de Lol, dit-on, fut alors marquée par des signes de souffrance. Mais qu'est-ce à dire qu'une souffrance sans sujet?" (23). (Lol's prostration, they said, was marked by signs of suffering. But what is a subjectless suffering?) Lol left her house one night and met a man whom she later married. A man whom she barely knew and who, it was rumored, expressed disquieting interest in young girls. They had three children and established themselves in the comfortable middle-class of Lol's home town of S. Tahla. But Lol remains oddly "absent."

Did Lol suffer while she silently watched Richardson dance with Stretter?

> Mais, elle, pour Lol. V. Stein, au départ, l'omission de la douleur, enfin, si vous voulez, cette espèce d'echec dans la tentative qu'elle a faite pour rejoindre l'amour du couple de Anne-Marie Stretter et de Richardson, elle a totalement échoué, c'est-à-dire que là aussi il y a un chaînon qui a manqué. La jalousie n'a pas été vécue.[17]

> But for her, for Lol. V. Stein, at the beginning, the absence of suffering, or, if you prefer, this kind of failure in the effort she made to join the love between Anne-Marie Stretter and Richardson, she failed completely, which is to say that there too a link was missing. She never lived out her jealousy.

Did her later silence camouflage an inner turmoil? Hold believes that Lol could never bring her suffering to language, could never find the words to tell the story of her pain, a pain that would have been mixed with pleasure had she imagined and penetrated the fantasy of a permanent presence to the couple that abandoned her.

> Mais ce qu'elle croit, c'est qu'elle devait y pénétrer, que c'était ce qu'il lui fallait faire, que ç'aurait été pour toujours, pour sa tête et pour son corps, leur plus grande douleur et leur plus grande joie confondues jusque dans leur définition devenue unique mais innommable faute d'un mot. . . . Ç'aurait été un mot-absence, un mot-trou, creusé en son centre d'un trou, de ce trou où tous les autres mots auraient été enterrés. On n'aurait pas pu le dire mais on aurait pu le faire résonner. Immense, sans fin, un gong vide, il aurait retenu ceux qui voulaient partir, il les aurait convaincus de l'impossible, il les aurait assourdis à tout autre vocable que lui-même, en une fois, il les aurait nommés, eux, l'avenir et l'instant. (53–54)

> But what she believes is that she was supposed to penetrate it, that that was what she was supposed to do, that it would have been forever, for her mind and for her body, their greatest pain and their greatest pleasure confused in their definition become one but unnameable for want of a word. It would have been a word-absence, a word-hole, hollowed in its center by a hole, by a hole where all other words would have been buried. It could not have been said but it could have resounded. Immense, endless, a hollow gong, it would have retained those who wanted to leave, it would have convinced them of the impossible, it would have deafened them to all other words but itself, in an instant, it would have named them, them, the future and the moment.

Hold undertakes a mission to supply the language for want of which, he imagines, Lol is silent. To discover the story, plot the events, and banish the effect of that traumatic moment that occurred ten years before the novel opens. Informed by his accommodating lover, Tatiana Karl, Lol's childhood friend and witness to Richardson's transformation and seduction as well as to Lol's devastation, Tatiana would seem a reliable informant. Hold's style is loosely psychological. This is to be the history of Lol's illness that organizes the past and will organize Hold's tale like a vanishing point does a painting. The ball is the source of the future that has sprung from it.

If Lol would be better known once the story of her past is told, knowledge is not its own reward. Hold's enterprise is far from disinterested. He loves Lol and believes that he can occupy a special place in her life, a privilege he covets. As Hold begins to trace Lol's movement through time from past to present, he discovers that his is no easy task. Lol is laconic and others' stories must be solicited. But others have little to say about T. Beach. "Lol, raconte madame Stein, fut ramenée à S. Tahla, et elle resta dans sa chambre, sans en sortir du tout, pendant quelques semaines" (23). (Lol, says Madame Stein, was brought back to S. Tahla, and she stayed in her room for weeks on end without ever going out) "Ainsi, si, de ce qui suit, Lol n'a parlé à personne, la gouvernante se souvient, elle, un peu . . ." (41). (Thus, if of what follows, Lol never spoke to anyone, the governess remembers a bit . . .) "Le récit de cette nuit-là fait par Jean Bedford à Lol elle-même contribue, il me semble, à son histoire récente. C'en sont là les derniers faits voyants. Après quoi ils disparaissent à peu près de cette histoire pendant dix ans" (26). (The story of that night told by Jean Bedford to Lol contributes, it seems to me, to her recent history. Those are the last conspicuous facts. After which they more or less disappear from this story for ten years.) Like an archaeologist assembling fragments of an artifact in the hope of reconstructing the object, Hold organizes the meager pieces. Without Lol's own commentary, however, and with little else to go on, Hold elaborates her story himself.[18]

His first effort produces a basic biography with a biological beginning and middle. "Lol Stein est née ici à S. Tahla et elle y a vécu une grande partie de sa jeunesse. Son père était professeur à l'Université. Elle a un frère plus âgé d'elle de neuf ans—je ne l'ai jamais vu—on dit qu'il vit à Paris. Ses parents sont morts" (9). (Lol Stein was born here in S. Tahla where she spent most of her youth. Her father was a professor at the University. She has a brother nine years older than she—I've never seen him—they say he lives in Paris. Her parents are dead.) Signed by an authoritative *je*, this autobiography situates Lol in a precise landscape and a curiously mother-less family. It is not Lol's birth that concerns Hold, however, but the ball, to which he accords the status of an originary trauma. The biography begins Lol's story prematurely. In the interest of finding the right genre—a case history—Hold freely jettisons the first years of Lol's life.

Les dix-neuf ans qui ont précédé cette nuit, je ne veux pas les connaître plus que je ne le dis, ou à peine, ni autrement que dans leur chronologie même s'ils recèlent une minute magique à laquelle je dois d'avoir connu Lol V. Stein. Je ne le veux pas parce que la présence de son adolescence dans cette histoire risquerait d'atténuer un peu aux yeux du lecteur l'écrasante actualité de cette femme dans ma vie. Je vais donc la chercher, je la prends là où je crois devoir le faire, au moment où elle me paraît commencer à bouger pour venir à ma rencontre, au moment précis où les dernières venues, deux femmes, franchissent la porte de la salle de bal du casino municipal de T. Beach. (12–13)

The nineteen years that preceded that night, I don't want to know them more than I say, or barely, other than chronologically even if they do contain the magic moment to which I owe my knowledge of Lol V. Stein. I do not want to because the presence of her adolescence in this story might diminish, in the reader's eyes, the crushing reality of this woman in my life. I am going to look for her, I take her there where I believe I should, at the moment where she seems to begin to move toward me, from the exact moment when the latecomers, two women, enter the door of the ballroom at the municipal casino in T. Beach.

Beginning anew his story of their crossing paths, Hold opens with the arrival of two women at the casino, Anne-Marie Stretter and her daughter. Lol begins to be who she is and to move toward him at the moment when the woman who supplants her enters the door. Hold's ardor shapes the uncluttered narrative line on which to hang his fiction. "Voici, tout au long, mêlés, à la fois, ce faux semblant que raconte Tatiana Karl et ce que j'invente sur la nuit du Casino de T. Beach. A partir de quoi je raconterai mon histoire de Lol V. Stein" (12). (Here, mixed together from beginning to end, are this misleading version that Tatiana tells and what I make up concerning the night of the Casino at T. Beach. Based on these I will tell my story of Lol V. Stein.)

Hold's fiction will not find favor with Tatiana, the eyewitness, friend, and primary informant. She sees things differently. "Tatiana, elle, ne croit pas au rôle prépondérant de ce fameux bal de T. Beach dans la maladie de Lol V. Stein. Tatiana Karl, elle, fait remonter plus avant, plus avant même que leur amitié, les origines de cette maladie" (10). (Tatiana does not believe in the centrality of this famous ball at T. Beach in the illness of Lol V. Stein. She, Tatiana Karl places its origins earlier, earlier even than their friendship.) T. Beach was not the trauma for Lol that Hold would like to believe; if it was a difficult moment it does not merit the status of the originary moment that Hold accords it. Not that Tatiana names an earlier cause for Lol's illness, nor is she invited to flesh out her disagreement. Her opinion, like Lol's early years, is jettisoned in order to facilitate the case history. The two characters, however, never engage in a prolonged diagnostic evaluation. But their impasse evokes the issue of causality as well as the place of desire in the construction of narrative.

Hold's focus on the ball as the cause of Lol's illness and key to her cure served his own interests. His strategy is clear. He must "cure" Lol and in order to do so he must know her. To know her, he must know when she began to be herself. His notion of causality and character formation are simple. Lol saw her lover leave with another woman and has never been the same since. We can hardly hold Duras's narrator to a rigorously Freudian notion of the psychogenesis of hysteria, nor of the logic and chronology of traumatic events.[19] To discern the trauma, to interpret the manifestation of its symptoms, and to characterize the evidence pointing to it are all complex tasks for the analyst. And from the outset, Hold is careful to sanction his version of Lol's story with her imagined consent.

Aplanir le terrain, le défoncer, ouvrir des tombeaux où Lol fait la morte, me paraît plus juste, du moment qu'il faut inventer les chaînons qui me manquent dans l'histoire de Lol V. Stein, que de fabriquer des montagnes, d'édifier des obstacles, des accidents. Et je crois, connaissant cette femme, qu'elle aurait préféré que je remédie dans ce sens à la pénurie des faits de sa vie. D'ailleurs c'est toujours à partir d'hypothèses non gratuites et qui ont déja, à mon avis, reçu un début de confirmation, que je le fais. (41)

To smooth over the landscape, delve into it, open the tombs where Lol pretends to be dead seems more correct to me, since I have to invent the links that are missing in Lol V. Stein's story, than inventing mountains, creating obstacles, interruptions. And I believe, knowing this woman, that she would have preferred that I remedy in this fashion the penury of facts about her life. Moreover, I always proceed from justified hypotheses which have, in my opinion, already begun to be confirmed.

The landscape imagery in this passage is striking and revealing. Lol is interred and Hold exhumes her body, returning her to the here and now so that she can embrace the present and Hold in it. For he has told us from the outset that she plays a significant role in his life, and that he must begin her story at the moment when she begins to move toward him—the ball. Hold's infatuation with Lol is intense from the novel's outset, but when he met her or why he wants to seduce her is unclear until page 85. Not an unusual move in a novel by Duras whose narratives are rarely linear.

Hold's case history is also an adventure story. His desire to meet and possess Lol shapes a fiction that resembles a folktale of the type described by Propp. The absent heroine is held in the thrall of her obsession with her past. This is the obstacle that Hold must overcome. Lol's obsession is of Hold's invention. He is both the hero and narrating consciousness of the tale of would-be liberation in which he wrests her from the powerful fascination with Richardson and Stretter.

Hold must learn to narrate the night of T. Beach. How was Lol ravished? What happened at the ball?

THE BALL SCENE

La femme la plus âgée s'était attardée un instant à regarder l'assistance puis elle s'était retournée en souriant vers la jeune fille qui l'accompagnait. Sans aucun doute possible celle-ci était sa fille. . . . Son élégance et dans le repos, et dans le mouvement, raconte Tatiana, inquiétait. Lol, frappée d'immobilité, avait regardé s'avancer, comme lui, cette grâce abandonnée, ployante, d'oiseau mort. . . . Qui était-elle? On le sut plus tard: Anne-Marie Stretter.
Lorsque Michael Richardson se tourna vers Lol et qu'il l'invita à danser pour la dernière fois de leur vie, Tatiana Karl l'avait trouvé pâli et sous le coup d'une préoccupation subite [et] envahissante qu'elle sut qu'il avait bien regardé, lui aussi, la femme qui venait d'entrer. . . . Il était devenue différent. . . . Michael Richardson se dirigea vers elle dans une émotion si intense qu'on prenait peur à l'idée qu'il aurait pu être éconduit. Lol, suspendue, attendit, elle aussi. La femme ne refusa pas. (13–17)

The older woman had paused for a moment to look at the crowd then she had looked back, smiling at the young girl who was with her. Without any

doubt whatsoever, this was her daughter. . . . Her elegance both while at rest and in motion, Tatiana says, were disquieting. Lol, as if struck by paralysis, had watched as he did, the advance of this woman dressed in black, whose unselfconscious yielding grace was like that of a dead bird. . . . Who was she? We learned later: Anne-Marie Stretter.
When Michael Richardson turned to invite Lol to dance with him for the last time in their lives, Tatiana had found him pale and stricken with a sudden and invasive preoccupation by which she understood that he too had looked at the woman who just entered. . . . He had changed. . . . Michael Richardson walked toward the woman with such intense emotion that we feared a false step. Lol, immobile waited, she also. . . . The woman did not refuse.

As written by Hold and remembered by Tatiana, the drama opens with the entry of Stretter and her daughter. Dressed in black, they arrive and pause; the stage is set for Richardson's transformation. Visibly marked upon seeing Stretter, he looks first at her and then back at Lol, soliciting permission to invite the newcomer to dance. With this gesture Richardson confirms the language of his adventure as visual. His look momentarily equates these two women. But only one will ultimately occupy his vision. Lol silently acquiesces to his wordless request. She will later reiterate this moment in the hope of maintaining an equilibrium which Richardson ruptures. The couple dances. Lol watches and is forgotten.

Voir l'amour qui se passe entre l'homme que l'on aime et soi-même, brutalement joué dehors, voir le regard qui fait votre être fixer sur un autre corps: une femme jalouse se voit, fascinée, transportée dans l'autre. Mise hors d'elle-même, défaite de ses repères, de son intimité.[20]

To see the love between the man one loves and oneself brutally played outside, to see the look that defines your entire being attach itself to another body: a jealous woman sees herself, fascinated and transported into the other. Exiled from herself, without bearings, without intimacy.

From this moment on, neither Richardson nor Stretter look at Lol who remains rooted to the spot. Her passion is played to the rhythm of an unnamed dance tune. The dance floor serves as the stage, but for whose fantasy? Is this the scenario of Lol's passion or is it Hold's?
The ricochet of looks among the three characters—Richardson looked at Stretter, then at Lol, Lol watches Stretter and Richardson, Stretter looks elsewhere—organizes the ball. Point of view becomes the equivalent of the place of each of the characters in this drama of

desire and exile. Lol's absorption in the spectacle is absolute, Hold claims. "Elle guettait l'événement, couvait son immensité, sa précision d'horlogerie. Si elle avait été l'agent même non seulement de sa venue mais de son succès, Lol n'aurait pas été plus fascinée" (17). (Lol watched the event, nurtured its immensity, its clocklike precision. If she had been the agent not only of its arrival but of its success, Lol couldn't have been more fascinated.) Unseen but seeing, Lol is stripped of consciousness of self; her lover forgets her, vacating the stage of her stare. When the couple leaves the casino, Lol therefore loses consciousness. "Lol resta toujours là où l'événement l'avait trouvée lorsque Anne-Marie Stretter était entrée, derrière les plantes vertes du bar. . . . Lol les suivit des yeux à travers les jardins. Quand elle ne les vit plus, elle tomba par terre, évanouie" (19, 22). (Lol stayed there where the event had found her when Anne-Marie Stretter had come in, behind the green plants at the bar. . . . Lol watched them as they crossed through the gardens. When she could no longer see them, she fell in a dead faint.) Hold believes—and this will be his undoing—that the ball is governed by a reciprocity of vision and intersubjectivity. You are known by those who see you; to be unseen is to cease to be. To cease to be desired. Richardson takes leave of Lol in a look and with it he replaces her with Stretter.

Lol recalls the apocalyptic drama of her youth whose final moments, in particular, claim her attention.

> [D]ans les multiples aspects du bal de T. Beach, c'est la fin qui retient Lol. C'est l'instant précis de sa fin, quand l'aurore arrive avec une brutalité inouïe et la sépare du couple que formaient Michael Richardson et Anne-Marie Stretter, pour toujours, toujours. Lol progresse chaque jour dans la reconstitution de cet instant. Elle arrive même à capter un peu de sa foudroyante rapidité, à l'étaler, à en grillager les secondes dans une immobilié d'une extrême fragilité mais qui est pour elle d'une grâce infinie.
> Elle se promène encore. Elle voit de plus en plus précisément, clairement ce qu'elle veut voir. Ce qu'elle rebâtit c'est la fin du monde. Elle se voit, et c'est là sa pensée véritable, à la même place, dans cette fin, toujours, au centre d'une triangulation dont l'aurore et eux deux sont les termes éternels. . . . (52)

> [O]f the many aspects of the dance at T. Beach, it's the end that fascinates Lol . . . the very moment of her end when the dawn arrives with a startling brutality and separates her forever, forever, from the couple of Michael Richardson and Anne-Marie Stretter. Lol moves forward daily in the reconstitution of this event. She is even able to capture its lightening rapidity, to slow it down, spread it out, entrap the seconds in a fragile

immobility which is, for her, of infinite grace. She walks through it again and sees more and more clearly what she wants to see. She reconstructs the end of the world. She sees herself . . . in the middle of a triangulation of which the dawn and the two of them are the eternal terms. . . .

In the triangle, Lol is both observer and participant.[21] Her visual fascination identifies her with the couple and denies her separation from them. Her absorption preserves her place in that moment before which the ball scene becomes a drama of exclusion. It is a memory that Duras describes as a cinema.

[L]'éternité du bal dans le cinéma de Lol V. Stein. . . . Lol progresse chaque jour dans la reconstitution de cet instant. . . . Et cela recommence; les fenêtres fermées, scellées, le bal muré dans la lumière nocturne les aurait contenus tous les trois et eux seuls. . . . Il aurait fallu murer le bal, en faire ce navire de lumière sur lequel chaque après-midi Lol s'embarque mais qui reste là, dans ce port impossible, à jamais amarré et prêt à quitter, avec ses trois passagers, tout cet avenir-ci dans lequel Lol V. Stein maintenant se tient. (55)

[T]he eternity of the ball in the cinema of Lol V. Stein. Lol daily progresses in the reconstruction of this instant. . . . And it begins again; the closed and sealed windows, the dance immured in the nocturnal light would have enveloped all three of them, and them alone. The dance would have had to be immured, made into this vessel of light on which each afternoon Lol embarks but remains, there in this impossible harbor, always anchored and ready to leave with its three passengers, this entire future in which Lol V. Stein now remains.

Hold can only write the definitive version of Lol's story once he dislodges her from her spectator's place in the cinema of her trauma. How will he historicize Lol's eternal memory? The ball occupies her memory; it is her film, her home. "Le bal reprend un peu de vie, frémit, s'accroche à Lol. Elle le réchauffe, le protège, le nourrit, il grandit, sort de ses plis, s'étire, un jour il est prêt. Elle y entre. Elle y entre chaque jour. . . . Et dans cette enceinte largement ouverte à son seul regard, elle recommence le passé, elle l'ordonne, sa véritable demeure, elle la range" (51). (The ball quivers, comes slowly to life, fastens itself to Lol. She warms it, protects it, nourishes it, it grows, unfolds, stretches, one day it is ready. She enters. She enters it daily. And in this enclosure, wide open only to her look, she starts the past over, she arranges it, her true domain, she organizes it.) A veritable fantasy this memory, which is marked by the characteristic presence of the spectator as well as the frame, which stands as a metaphor for the eye which watched the troubling scene.[22] Lol's fantasy will prove to be a structure in which a newly ravished spectator will take up residency in one of the designated places.[23]

By editing her memory of the ball, Lol would escape her total eclipse by Stretter. She claims not to understand who is in her place, the place of Richardson's lover. "Je ne comprends pas qui est à ma place" (160). No one can take her place. The economy of substitution and replacement in which someone replaces her is impossible. Lol rejects the process of exchange which displaces and replaces her. She will not become a placeholder, will not take up a place in a system of sexual difference. She hesitates, then, between identifying with Stretter and accepting the difference between them. Is the ball scene traumatic, then, because it recalls another difference, that violent differentiation made between mothers and their offspring of the same sex, a violent rejection of the first object of identification?[24] Stretter, the text takes the trouble to inform us, is a mother who enters the casino in the company of her daughter. If she is central to this trauma, it is as a maternal sexual body. Is Lol's persistent "return" to the ball a wish for mastery over this event which recalls another, earlier trauma?

To ask such a question and to employ terms like *place* and *economy* when speaking of subjectivity, evokes Lacanian categories of the "Imaginary" and the "Symbolic." To argue that Lol's refusal to acknowledge another woman suggests an archaic stage of relations in which an illusion of identification and of nondifferentiation are dominant. The earliest form of this relationship is that between mother and child. It occurs at a moment when a baby barely distinguishes itself from its mother. Lacan calls this stage the "Imaginary," in part because the identification is made visually. The baby does not perceive itself as a distinct entity from its mother, the source of nourishment and pleasure. In the mirror stage, roughly corresponding to the age of eighteen months, which has become the exemplary expression of the Imaginary, Lacan claims that the baby's self-(mis)identification is made with an image.[25] A false identification is projected between an image of independence and maturity and a more greatly limited physical prowess. By contrast with the Imaginary, the "Symbolic" designates a mode of intersubjective relationships characterized by difference rather than identity. It is not a fundamentally visual relationship based on identification with another or with an image of a misrecognized self, but rather introduces a third term into the equation, an other, or the other. The frontiers and passage between the Imaginary and the Symbolic are highly elusive. Vestiges of the Imaginary persist in the Symbolic. These terms are evoked here as suggestions for approaching Lol as she appears suspended between a visual universe and one of language, and of the tension that Duras so frequently establishes between her heroines' desire for visual presence and identification, and her narrators' drive to narrativize. But what of the specificity of Stretter as a maternal and sexual figure?

THE FEMININE BODY AS A TRAUMATIC SITE

Il est à prendre à la première scène, où Lol est de son amant proprement dérobée, c'est à dire, qu'il est à suivre dans le thème de la robe, lequel ici supporte le fantasme où Lol s'attache le temps d'après, d'un au-delà dont elle n'a pas su trouver le mot, ce mot, qui, refermant les portes sur eux trois, l'eût conjointe au moment où son amant eût enlevé la robe, la robe noire de la femme et dévoilé so nudité.[26]

We should begin with the first scene, when Lol is concealed from her lover, which is to say that the theme of the dress underpins the fantasy to which Lol attaches herself the next time, of a beyond for which she cannot find the word, this word which, shutting the doors on the three of them, would have joined her to them at the moment when her lover would have removed the dress, the woman's black dress, and revealed her nudity.

The blind spot of Hold's fantasy of Lol's trauma is Stretter's body. She is never completely unveiled; the site of the repressed is marked by this concealment.

Cet arrachement très ralenti de la robe de Anne-Marie Stretter, cet anéantissement de velours de sa propre personne, Lol n'a jamais réussi à le mener à son terme. . . . L'homme de T. Beach n'a plus qu'une tâche à accomplir, toujours la même dans l'univers de Lol: Michael Richardson, chaque après-midi, commence à dévêtir une autre femme que Lol et lorsque d'autres seins apparaissent, blancs, sous le fourreau noir, il en reste là, ébloui, un Dieu lassé par cette mise à nu, sa tâche unique, et Lol attend vainement qu'il la reprenne, de son corps infirme de l'autre elle crie, elle attend en vain, elle crie en vain. (56–57)

This very slow wrenching of Anne-Marie Stretter's dress, this velvet extinction of her own body, Lol has never been able to bring it to term. . . . The man from T. Beach has only a single task to accomplish, always the same in Lol's universe: Michael Richardson, each afternoon, begins to undress another woman and when other breasts appear, white beneath the black sheath, he stops, overwhelmed, a god tired of this denuding, his sole task, and Lol vainly waits for him to take her back, from her body of the other she shouts, she waits vainly, she shouts in vain.

Lol and Stretter are initially poised in a visual equilibrium; they share Richardson's gaze. One gaze, two bodies. As Stretter's body becomes visible, Lol's, inevitably, becomes invisible. Stretter's complete visibility—her nudity—means Lol's total eclipse. In order for the two bodies to remain visible, the fantasy must remain unfinished. The metaphors of illumination and eclipse underscore the centrality of vision here.

Il l'aurait dévêtue de sa robe noire avec lenteur et le temps qu'il l'eût fait une grande étape du voyage aurait été franchie.
J'ai vu Lol se dévêtir, inconsolable encore, inconsolable.
Il n'est pas pensable pour Lol qu'elle soit absente de l'endroit où ce geste a eu lieu. Ce geste n'aurait pas eu lieu sans elle: elle est avec lui chair à chair, forme à forme, les yeux scellés à son cadavre. Elle est née pour le voir. D'autres sont nés pour mourir. . . . (55)
Le corps long et maigre de l'autre femme serait apparu peu à peu. Et dans une progression rigoureusement parallèle et inverse, Lol aurait été remplacée par elle auprès de l'homme de T. Beach. Remplacée par cette femme, au souffle près. Lol retient ce souffle: à mesure que le corps de la femme apparaît à cet homme, le sien s'efface, s'efface, volupté, du monde. (56)

He would have undressed her slowly, taken off her black dress and in the time that he would have done so, a large portion of the journey would have been made.
I have seen Lol undress, unconsolable still, unconsolable.
Lol could not imagine being absent from the place where this gesture would take place. It could not happen without her: she is with it in her very skin, in her bones, her eyes sealed on its corpse. She was born to see it. Others are born to die. . . .
The long, thin body of the other woman would appear slowly. And in a rigorously parallel and inverse progression, Lol would have been replaced by her in her relation with the man from T. Beach. Replaced by this woman, even to her very breath. Lol holds this breath: as the body of the woman emerges into this man's sight, hers is effaced, effaced, delectation, from the world.

Lol's fantasy vigilance is eternal and it is within this eternity that the ball unfolds. Hold's version of her memory and her fantasy equate the unspeakable scandal with a woman's body: the replacement of Lol's body with that of another woman. Anne-Marie Stretter. Everything stops with the "indicible nudité d'un corps qui remplace le sien. Là tout s'arrête" (unspeakable nudity of the body that displaces her own. There, everything stops).[27]

Trauma, memory, and narration converge on the maternal body as a sexual body, a body that eclipses Lol's. In Lol's fantasy, neither the body nor its sexuality can be fully visible, nor can either be represented. Whose trauma, whose memory and whose scenario designate a feminine body as the site of narrative impasse? Whose trauma blocks Stretter's body from view? As Hold's narrative falters, he takes up his place in Lol's fantasy; he enters the structure that gives him a place from which he believes he can tell her story. This place, however, only subjects him to the logic of the ball. For Lol's fantasy imposes a structure in which the places are stable and only the placeholders shift. Ravished Hold.

OF UNTELLABLE TALES: SHOW OR TELL?

Lest we imagine that Lol is a passive victim of her early trauma, Roland Barthes reminds us that the ravished play an active role.

> Ravissement: épisode réputé initial (mais il peut être reconstruit après coup) au cours duquel le sujet amoureux se trouve "ravi" (capturé et enchanté) par l'image de l'objet aimé (nom populaire: *coup de foudre;* nom savant: *énamoration.*) Cependant, curieux chassé-croisé: dans le mythe ancien, le ravisseur est actif, il veut saisir sa proie, il est sujet du rapt (dont l'objet est une Femme, comme chacun sait, toujours passive); dans le mythe moderne (celui de l'amour-passion), c'est le contraire: le ravisseur ne veut rien, ne fait rien; il est immobile (comme une image), et c'est l'objet ravi qui est le vrai sujet de rapt.[28]

> Ravishing: a reputedly initial episode (but one which can be reconstructed after the fact) during the course of which the amorous subject is ravished (captivated or enchanted) by the image of the beloved object. (Popularly known as love at first sight: scholarly name: enamoration.) There is however, a curious crossover: in the myth, the ravisher is active and wants to seize the prey, the agent of the rape whose object is a Woman, always, as everyone knows, passive); in the modern myth of passion (that of love-passion), this situation is reversed. The ravisher wants nothing, does nothing, is immobile (like a picture) and it is the ravished object who is the veritable subject of the rape.

Hold becomes a player after crossing the narrative frame to enter into what he believes to be Lol's visual universe. He identifies with her, believing that he will thus see things from her point of view. His initiation begins chez Tatiana when Lol, after many years, visits her old friend. Hold believes that he alone holds the key to Lol's inexplicable visit. "J'étais le seul à savoir, à cause de ce regard immense, famélique qu'elle avait eu pour moi en embrassant Tatiana, qu'il y avait une raison précise a sa présence ici" (90). (I was the only one to know, because of the immense and famished way which she looked at me while kissing Tatiana, that there was a precise reason for her presence here.) Attentive to Lol's looks, which he interprets as stage directions, Hold takes up a position in the space established by her gaze. "Elle veut . . . être rencontrée par moi et vue par moi dans un certain espace qu'elle aménage en ce moment" (122). (She wants . . . to be met by me and seen by me in a certain space that she is arranging at this moment.) Sensitive to the architectural frames in which Lol places herself and those around her, Hold believes that he understands that Lol's is a gesture of repetition, a replay of the ricochet of gazes that excluded her at the ball and one in which he must take up a place if he is to gain access to the fantasy space she inhabits.

> Une place est à prendre, qu'elle n'a pas réussi à avoir à T. Beach, il y a dix ans. Où? Elle ne vaut pas celle d'opéra de T. Beach. Laquelle? Il faudra bien se contenter de celle-ci pour arriver enfin à se frayer un passage, à avancer un peu plus vers cette rive lointaine où ils habitent, les autres. Vers quoi? Quelle est cette rive? (70)

> There is a place to be had that she did not manage to have at T. Beach ten years ago. Where? It's not as good as the opera box at T. Beach. Which one? This one must suffice for now in order to finally cut a path, to go forward a bit more toward that distant shore that they inhabit, those others. Towards what? What is this shore?

Lol's first frame-up operates like a cinematic establishing shot. She and Tatiana are engaged in intimate conversation as they stand flanked by draped glass doorways. Hold is to watch them, to be the spectator who at once understands their intimacy and his exclusion.

> Lol caresse toujours les cheveux de Tatiana. D'abord elle la regarde intensément puis son regard s'absente, elle caresse en aveugle qui veut reconnaître. . . . Lol lève les yeux et je vois ses lèvres prononcer Tatiana Karl. Elle a un regard opaque et doux. Ce regard qui était pour Tatiana tombe sur moi: elle m'aperçoit derrière la baie. Tatiana ne s'aperçoit de rien. Elle fait quelques pas vers Tatiana, elle l'enlace légèrement et, insensiblement, elle l'amène à la porte-fenêtre qui donne sur le parc. Elle l'ouvre. J'ai compris. (107)

Lol is still stroking Tatiana's hair. At first she looks at her intensely and then her gaze goes elsewhere, she continues to stroke her hair mechanically like a blind person trying to recognize something. Lol raises her eyes and I see her lips pronounce "Tatiana Karl." Her look is gentle and opaque. The look that was for Tatiana falls on me; she sees me behind the window but Tatiana sees nothing. She takes a few steps toward Tatiana, gently slips her arm around her and guides her almost imperceptibly toward the window that looks out onto the garden. She opens the window. I understand.

What has Hold understood? That Lol wants to be seen. Hold understands the equations of seeing and being, of being and being desired. He solicits Lol's gaze, hopeful that being seen by her he will be desired by her. "Je voulais revoir ses yeux sur moi. . . . Elle me regarda, comme je le désirais" (96). (I wanted to see her eyes on me again. She looked at me, as I desired.) His desire reiterates Lol's own. Hold believes that he understands Lol, and that they now see things from the same vantage point. "[E]lle veut voir venir avec moi, s'avancer sur nous, nous engloutir, l'obscurité de demain qui sera celle de la nuit de T. Beach" (121). (She wants to watch with me the darkness of tomorrow which will be that of the night of T. Beach, wants to watch it come, move toward us, swallow us.) But does he understand Lol's caress? Does he understand that Lol's place places him in a circuit of looks and desires that is already determined, and that he does not redetermine, but rather repeats?

Hold becomes a willing actor in Lol's drama. At the Hôtel du Bois he observes Lol's most spectacular replay of the ball scene. The scene is recounted in the peculiar tense in which the entire novel is written, one that blurs chronology just as it blurs the distinction between fantasmatic invention and memory. On the outskirts of S. Tahla, in a hotel to which Lol herself came with Richardson, Hold stands at the window of his lit room. Tatiana is in the room. This is their trysting spot. Lol has followed them to the hotel, awaiting nightfall in order, recounts Hold, to "se nourrir, dévorer ce spectacle inexistant, invisible, la lumière d'une chambre où d'autres sont" (72) (nourish herself, devour this nonexistent and invisible spectacle, the light of a bedroom in which others are). Speaking of himself in the third person, referring to himself as the man, Hold describes the scene, plays to Lol who watches, blindly, as he invites Tatiana to the window, placing her squarely within the framed and well-lit opening. Glowing in the night, the window resembles nothing so much as a drive-in movie screen on which is projected—but by whom? Lol's fantasy, the fiction of Lol's fantasy as Hold conceives it.

> L'ombre de l'homme passe à travers le rectangle de lumière. Une première fois, puis une deuxième fois, en sens inverse. . . . La lumière se modifie, elle devient plus forte. Elle ne vient plus du fond, à gauche de la fenêtre, mais du plafond. . . . Tatiana Karl, à son tour, nue dans sa chevelure noire, traverse la scène de lumière, lentement. C'est peut-être dans le rectangle de vision de Lol qu'elle s'arrête. Elle se tourne vers le fond où l'homme doit être.
>
> La fenêtre est petite et Lol ne doit voir des amants que le buste coupé à la hauteur du ventre. Ainsi ne voit-elle pas la fin de la chevelure de Tatiana. (74)

> The man's shadow crosses through the rectangle of light. A first time, then a second time, in the opposite direction. . . . The light changes, it becomes stronger. It no longer comes from the back, to the left of the window, but from overhead. Tatiana Karl, in her turn, naked in her black hair, crosses the stage of light, slowly. It is, perhaps, in the rectangle which is visible to Lol that Tatiana stops. She turns towards the back of the room, where the man is supposed to be.
>
> The window is small and cuts off Lol's sight of the lovers from the belly up. Thus, she cannot see the end of Tatiana's hair.

This scene recalls the earlier ball scene. An equation is established between Tatiana and Stretter. Tatiana, like Stretter, is sheathed in black. The black sheath is lifted to reveal—but only partially—her nude body. As Lol watches Stretter in fantasy, and Tatiana at the window, the female body—focus of her gaze—is only incompletely visible. The window frame cuts Tatiana off from full view; the end of her hair is out of sight just as her body is not visible from the belly down. Lol's vision like her fantasy of Richardson's undressing of Stretter, which stops at the moment when he is dazzled by her white breasts so that she is never completely disrobed, occults that which it cannot bear to see. The sexual feminine body. The sex of the feminine body remains invisible. Intolerable sexuality, intolerable, unrepresentable. Is this the unassimilable element of Lol's trauma?[29] While the framing and barring from vision of parts of the other woman's body marks the site of Lol's trauma, it assures her place as spectator. The frame implies her vision so long as it represses what cannot be symbolized. Moreover, the frames—the windows, the doorways, the narrative—are themselves a metaphor for a gaze, a steady focus upon, and repression of, what cannot be seen.[30] So long as the other woman does not completely displace her, Lol retains her place, her delicious place in the moment of the translation into pure vision of her self. This same eviction which Hold, desirous of occupying Lol's place, will suffer.

> Il devait y avoir une heure que nous étions là tous les trois, qu'elle nous avait vus tour à tour apparaître dans l'encadrement de la fenêtre, ce miroir qui ne reflétait rien et devant lequel elle devait délicieusement ressentir l'éviction souhaitée de sa personne. (143)

> There must have been an hour when we were there all three, that she had seen us one by one appear in the frame of the window, this mirror which reflected nothing and in front of which she must have reveled in the desired eviction of her person.

Can we distinguish Lol's fantasy from Hold's narration of her fantasy, his own fantasy? His narrative desire to tell Lol's story, like his will to be seen by Lol and to see from her place, subjects him to the logic of her place. But if he is there, as Lol was, he is ravished. Ravishing Lol ravishes Hold by situating him within the circuit of looks and desires that reiterate her displacement without arresting it. If Hold has understood Lol's desires, he has not been able to definitively recount her tale, nor has he been able to play out her passion. Rather, he has taken up a place in a dramatic and silent reiteration of her trauma; there is no narrative cure here for Lol, there is only a circulation among places and ongoing fascination of her drama.[31] The logic of Lol's fantasy is to perturb Hold's narration; the logic of his narration is to displace her fantasy; the logic of Duras's text is to play off the visual fascination of fantasy against the imposition of narrative order.

Narrative Perturbation: Disrupted Perspective and Repetition

Duras recounts a tale of obsessive memory and does so obsessively. The novel is shaped by repetitions that are not only thematic, of the dance scene, for example, but narrative.[32] The actors in this drama of subjectivity occupy the different designated places in it. Point of view is a function of the rotating place of character and taleteller. The fantasy dominating the novel structures narrative organization. Therefore, what we might describe as the narrative perturbation of the text should be taken as exemplary of the rhetoric of fantasy, understood as both a scene and script. Narrative logic, this perturbation, this slow destabilization that includes impossible points of view as well as the disintegration of the narrating subject, characterizes this fantasy text.

Several shifts in narrative voice suggest that narrative destabilization mimes the logic of Lol's fantasy that is, lest we forget, the fantasy of a consciousness reduced to a gaze, a delicious eviction of being. For the first fifty pages of the novel (pp. 9–58), an anonymous first-person pronoun, *je*, situates itself in the *ici* of Lol's geographic space. Lol's biography is presented in an uncomplicated and direct style. In the next fifty pages, however, the narrative voice shifts; the tale is told from a third-person point of view. "Prudente, calculeuse [Lol], marche assez loin derrière lui. Lorsqu'il suit des yeux une autre femme, elle baisse la tête ou se retourne légèrement" (62). (Careful, calculating, she walks at a distance behind him. When he watches another woman go by, she lowers her head or turns, slightly.) Who is he? Why is Lol following him? What has become of the *je* of the first section? Several pages later, "Tatiana présente à Lol Pierre Beugner, son mari, et Jacques Hold, un de leurs amis, la distance est couverte, moi" (85). (Tatiana introduces Lol to Pierre Beugner, her husband, and Jacques Hold, one of their friends, the distance is covered, me.) What distance has been covered? This pronominal collision, the equivalent of a cinematic zoom, covers the "distance" between *il* and *je*. Hold's *moi* momentarily sutures the space separating narrator from character, just as Lol's vision would suture the distance between her and the couple, the object of her gaze. Narration and story converge as Hold is poised at the narrative frame, at the intersection between the tale and its telling.

The verbal collision of narrator and character does not result in any stable perspective, however. Rather, the narrative voice begins to oscillate more and more quickly between first- and third-person voices. As if imitating Lol's double role as character and spectator in her fantasy, Hold dances between the two places of narrator and character in his story. Duras's novel offers a veritable demonstration of the dynamics of the fantasy as it disrupts the tale that Hold attempts to recount, and the stability of the narrative voice.

Two different passages will serve as examples of the destabilization

of point of view that accompanies the storyteller's enmeshment in
Lol's fantasy.

> Votre chambre s'est éclairée et j'ai vu Tatiana qui passait dans la lumière.
> Elle était nue sous ses cheveux noirs. Elle ne bouge pas, les yeux sur le
> jardin, elle attend. Elle vient de dire que Tatiana est nue sous ses cheveux
> noirs. Cette phrase est encore la dernière qui a été prononcée. J'entends:
> "nue sous ses cheveux noirs, nue, nue, cheveux noirs." Les deux derniers
> mots surtout sonnent avec une égale et étrange intensité. Il est vrai que
> Tatiana était ainsi que Lol vient de la décrire, nue sous ses cheveux noirs.
> Elle était ainsi dans la chambre fermée, pour son amant. (134–35)

> Your room was lit and I saw Tatiana who was moving into the light. She
> was naked beneath her black hair. She doesn't move, her eyes on the
> garden, she waits. She just said that Tatiana is naked beneath her black
> hair. This sentence is still the last one to have been spoken. I hear: "naked
> under her black hair, naked, naked, black hair." The last two words
> especially ring with an equal and strange intensity. It is true that Tatiana
> was as Lol just described her, naked under her black hair. She was thus in
> the closed bedroom, for her lover.

Hold's narrative incorporates as unattributed direct discourse Lol's
account of another scene, one in which she observes Hold. But from
what place does Hold now tell this? The passage demonstrates a
process of narrative digestion that suggests the collapse of language as
a support for any meaning whatsoever, a collapse that occurs, not
innocently, when the would-be referent is Tatiana's body. Hold does
not simply restate Lol's phrase. He decomposes and rephrases it,
repeating pieces of it, as if to better isolate them, unable to narratize.
Nude Tatiana sheathed in black defies the narrative enterprise, overwhelming Hold just as Stretter's unsheathing arrested an earlier narration. Language falters and explodes to become deafening sound; the
narrative encounters its limits at the precise place where Lol's fantasy
faltered—at the sight of a woman's nude body.

> L'intensité de la phrase augmente tout à coup. L'air a claqué autour d'elle,
> la phrase éclate, elle crève le sens. J'entends avec une force assourdissante
> et je ne la comprends pas, je ne comprends même plus qu'elle ne veut rien
> dire. . . . La nudité de Tatiana déjà nue grandit dans une surexposition qui
> la prive toujours davantage du moindre sens possible. Le vide est statue.
> Le socle est là: la phrase. Le vide est Tatiana nue sous ses cheveux noirs, le
> fait. Il se transforme, se prodigue, le fait ne contient plus le fait. . . . La
> voici, Tatiana Karl nue sous ses cheveux, soudain, entre Lol V. Stein et
> moi. (134–35)

The intensity of the words increases and suddenly the air around them explodes, the sentence explodes, it explodes all meaning. I hear it with a deafening force and I do not understand it any more than I understand that it is meaningless. Already Tatiana's nakedness expands in such a way that it loses meaning. Emptiness is the statue and the sentence is the pedestal. The emptiness is Tatiana, naked beneath her black hair, the fact. The fact is transformed and spreads out, it no longer contains itself, Tatiana naked beneath her black hair suddenly stands between me and Lol V. Stein.

Tatiana's nudity is the fact before which Hold's language falters. Is this the trauma at the center of the fantasy? Whose trauma? Whose fantasy has overwhelmed language become sound?

Tatiana enlève ses vêtements et Jacques Hold la regarde, regarde avec intérêt celle qui n'est pas son amour. A chaque vêtement tombé il reconnaît toujours davantage ce corps insatiable dont l'existence lui est indifférente. Il a déjà exploré ce corps, il le connaît mieux que Tatiana elle-même. Il regarde longuement cependant ces clairières d'un blanc qui se nuance au contour des formes. . . . Il la regarde jusqu'à perdre de vue l'identité de chaque forme, de toutes les formes, et même du corps entier. (155)

Tatiana takes off her clothes and Jacques Hold watches with interest the one who is not his beloved. With each piece of clothing, he further rcognizes this insatiable body whose very existence is unimportant. He has already explored this body, he knows it better even than Tatiana herself. Nonetheless, he carefully observes her white skin as it changes tone over the contours of her body. He watches her until he loses sight of the shape of each individual part of her, until he loses sight of the body altogether.

Tatiana's body slowly and progressively vanishes. Not only does her nudity perturb Hold's narrative, but it overwhelms his vision as well. The woman's body is the blinding and blind spot of narration. And as is so typically the case in Duras's writing, the evocation of sexuality is accompanied by violence. "Il cache le visage de Tatiana Karl sous le drap et ainsi il a son corps décapité sous la main: (156). (He hides Tatiana Karl's face beneath the sheet and in this way has her decapitated body under his hand.) Tatiana's body decapitated, Tatiana becomes a talking head that speaks from beneath the sheets and pronounces Lol's name. Tatiana's body is mutilated and cut off from view not just once, but twice. The window frame at the Hôtel du Bois cut her off from Lol's full view and now the bedsheet separates body from head. The sight of the female body is intolerable, but for whom? Within the destabilizing circulation of characters among places and looks that govern this novel, can the fantasy be discerned from memory? Can the fantasy fiction be attributed to any character at all? Characteristic of Duras's writing, the spectacle of feminine sexuality both thwarts and excites the narrative impulse, reveals the limits of narration to represent the spectacle, and forces her to move beyond language to cinema.

The instability of Hold's narrative perspective, the uncertainty of any coherent, nameable narrator, the tension between the narrative enterprise and narrated scene, attest to the novel's architecture as fantasmatic. The repetitions in the text confirm the obsessional quality of the fantasy. The terse biography with which the novel opens, for example, is repeated with some variation more than one hundred pages later.

C'est à S. Tahla que Lol a vécu toute sa jeunesse, ici, son père était d'origine allemande, il était professeur d'histoire à l'Université, sa mère était de S. Tahla, Lol a un frère de neuf ans plus âgé qu'elle, il vit à Paris, elle ne parle pas de ce seul parent, Lol a rencontré l'homme de T. Beach pendant les vacances scolaires d'été, un matin, aux courts, il avait vingt-cinq ans, fils unique de grands propriétaires des environs, sans emploi, cultivé, brillant, très brillant, d'humeur sombre, Lol dès qu'elle l'a vu a aimé Michael Richardson. (119)

Lol spent her entire youth here, in S. Tahla, her father came from a German background, he was a history professor at the University, her mother was from S. Tahla, Lol has a brother who is nine years older than she, he lives in Paris, she does not speak about her only relative, Lol met the man from T. Beach during a summer school vacation, one morning, at the tennis courts, he was twenty-five years old, the only son of rich landowners from this area, unemployed, cultured, brilliant, very brilliant, a dark-humored man, Lol loved Michael Richardson as soon as she laid eyes on him.

The second biography spills forth in a breathless run-on sentence, amplifying the first version that focused on Lol's immediate family, by including Lol's initial encounter with Richardson. What the biography leaves out, however, is noteworthy: No first person signs this version. Do the facts speak for themselves? The facts of Lol's story that emerged in the novel after its *incipit* are assimilated into this second version of her biography that has repositioned itself as if to better tell Lol's story. Where is Hold?

A second example of this process of repetition/modification describes an incident from Lol's childhood. Tatiana recounts:

> Elles, on les laissait faire, dit Tatiana, elles étaient charmantes, elles savaient mieux que les autres demander cette faveur, on la leur accordait. On danse, Tatiana? Une radio dans un immeuble voisin jouait des danses démodées.—une émission souvenir—dont elles se contentaient. Les surveillants envolvés, seules dans le grand préau où ce jour-là, entre les danses, on entendait le bruit des rues, allez Tatiana, allez viens, on danse Tatiana, viens. (19)

> Them, they left them alone, says Tatiana, they were charming girls, they knew better than the other girls how to ask for this favor and they got what they wanted. Shall we dance, Tatiana? A radio in a neighboring building was playing old dance music—a golden oldies broadcast—with which they were happy. The monitors were gone, [Tatiana and Lol were], alone in the courtyard where, that day, between dances, the noise from the streets could be heard, come on Tatiana, come on, let's dance, come on.

Eighty pages later:

> Le jeudi, Tatiana raconte, elles deux refusaient de sortir en rangs avec le collège. Elles dansaient dans le préau vide—on danse Tatiana!—un pick-up dans un immeuble voisin, toujours le même, jouait des danses anciennes—une émission souvenir qu'elles attendaient, les surveillants était envolées, seules dans l'immense cour du collège où on entendait ce jour-là, les bruits des rues. Allez, Tatiana, on danse. (98–99)

> On Thursdays, Tatiana says, the two of them refused to march out with the rest of the students, they danced in the empty courtyard—shall we dance, Tatiana?—a record player in a neighboring building, always the same one, played old dance tunes—an oldies but goodies show that they were awaiting, the monitors had gone off, [Tatiana and Lol were] alone in the immense school courtyard where, that day, could be heard the street noises. Come on Tatiana, let's dance.

This repetition of the dance scene, stylistically similar to the repetition of Lol's biography, is long and breathless as it tumbles forth, mixing direct dialogue and description. There is some reason to linger over this example not only because it repeats an earlier piece of the narration, but also because it is a variant of the most often-repeated scene in the novel—the ball scene. The notable difference here is that this isolated and intimate couple is feminine. Is the ball scene thus to be reinterpreted through another lens? Was this friendship the "earlier event" to which Tatiana alludes when speaking of the origins of Lol's illness? Does this scene, in its insistence, challenge the status of the ball scene as an originary trauma?

Lol and Tatiana, Hold had already observed, resemble each other. "Elles portent toutes deux ce soir des robes sombres qui les allongent, les font plus minces, moins différentes l'une de l'autre, peut-être, aux yeux des hommes" (170). (They are both wearing dark dresses this evening which make them look taller, slimmer, less different one from the other, in men's eyes.) Their similarity facilitates the possibility of the substitution, one for the other. More, they, like Stretter, wear dark dresses. They are, in the eyes of men, in Hold's eyes, similar. This similarity will be reasserted as identity when Lol names herself Tatiana Karl during her pilgrimage with Hold to T. Beach. Making love with him, she asks that he name her. "Elle gémit, me demande de le dire. Je dis: Tatiana Karl, par exemple" (218). (She moans, asks me to say it. I say, "Tatiana Karl, for example.") "Après, dans les cris, elle a insulté, elle a supplié, imploré qu'on la reprenne et qu'on la laisse à la fois . . . et il n'y a plus eu de différence entre elle et Tatiana Karl sauf dans ses yeux exempts de remords et dans la désignation qu'elle faisait d'elle-même—Tatiana ne se nomme pas, elle—et dans les deux noms qu'elle se donnait: Tatiana Karl et Lol V. Stein" (219). (Afterward, in her cries, she insulted, she begged, she implored that she be taken again and left at the same time . . . and there was no longer any difference between her and Tatiana Karl except in her remorseless eyes and in the way she named herself—Tatiana, she does not name herself—and in the two names she gave herself: Tatiana Karl and Lol V. Stein.) What does Lol enact in this self-re-nomination? She takes a name that does not name her, a gesture, an effort to identify with the woman who displaced her? Lol cannot occupy the place of sexuality in her own name. Hold falters. What biography can be written for a character thus dispossessed? His hope for a cure foiled, Hold wonders, "Je suis, je serais donc dupé par sa folie même?" (176). (Am I, could I be, duped by Lol's madness?)

The novel ends at the Hôtel du Bois where Hold and Tatiana again tryst while Lol lies in the rye fields, a blind spectator, a place holder enabling the replay of the scene that dislodges and anchors her. The circulation of characters in the fantasy of identity and difference set in motion by the trauma of the sexual feminine body escapes Hold's narrative frame; the frame that reiterates Lol's gaze at the ball similarly excises that which it did not see and cannot imagine. Stretter and Tatiana overwhelm language, vision, and imagination. The sexual feminine body remains the blinding and destabilizing center of *Le Ravissement de Lol V. Stein.*

3

Le Vice-consul and *India Song:* Dolores Mundi

Les personnages évoqués dans cette histoire ont été délogés du livre intitulé *Le Vice-consul* et projetées dans de nouvelles régions narratives.

—*India Song,* p. 9

Le Vice-consul reconjugates many themes as well as several formal devices dear to Duras. The anonymous narrator does not identify with any particular point of view or character. Within the cast of characters, another narrator, a male writer, is in the process of writing an imagined biography of a mad beggar-woman cast into exile by her mother. His framed narrative is set within the primary diegesis and erodes the boundaries between story and plot. Tale-telling, as is so often the case in Duras's work, grows from the desire to appropriate and domesticate experience, here, the attempt of colonial whites to participate in the suffering of India, to both know and deflect its horrors. The eponymous hero of the novel grapples with his inexplicably painful visions, is unable to give them verbal form, and is overcome by his passion for Anne-Marie Stretter in whom he sees a partner of the soul. His scream is the language closest to his desires; he never covers the distance between himself and Stretter, however. He is repugnant to the consulary world of which he is an unsettling member. A white leper, his exile and future in the administration are the main preoccupations of the French Consul.

The film, *India Song,* retains the diegetic universe and cast of characters of *Le Vice-consul*—indeed there are direct citations from the novel—with some important differences. The beggar-woman of the novel is only a voice on the sound track in the film. The voices recall Lol's story—uttering several sentences from the novel by way of which Duras was obliged to pass before making *India Song*[1]—and Stretter's seduction of Richardson at the ball is said to be the originary moment of their couple. Stretter is the visual center of the film in which Duras kills her off.[2] The ambassadorial reception occupies a major portion of the film's visuals but is only one of the short "chapters" in the novel. Where the novel sets storytelling *en abîme* by using the biography of the beggar-woman to erode the edges between the novel and its framed narrative, the most visually arresting of the Indian Cycle films multiplies and dislocates visual and narrative frames. There is a constant play of door frames, window frames, picture frames, and mirrors; mirrored space disrupts temporal and spatial signposts. Most importantly, the sound track is un-synchronized with the images. Sound track and images clearly rele-gate the narrative universe of *Le Vice-consul* to the past tense in *India Song*. Taken together, these two works allow us to explore what Marie-Claire Ropars has called the "circulation défective de [c]es textes," as Duras explores the new narrative regions offered in the cinema.[3]

Le Vice-consul

"Elle marche, écrit Peter Morgan" (9). (She walks, writes Peter Morgan) reads the first line of the novel. Peter Morgan, a white man in Calcutta is writing a biography. His biography, of another character in the novel, begins with an exile. She is a young peasant, pregnant, unmarried, and about to be banished from her family and home. Her expatriation is more correctly an exmatriation, for her mother issues the order that she lose herself in a place where nothing is familiar and everything is hostile. Inflexible, the mother warns her daughter not to return. "Si tu reviens, a dit la mère, je mettrai du poison dans ton riz pour te tuer" (10). (If you return, said her mother, I will put poison in your rice to kill you.) The young girl comes to envisage her exile as a road of maternal abandonment. "Dans la lumière bouillante et pâle, l'enfant encore dans le ventre, elle s'éloigne, sans crainte. Sa route, elle est sûre, est celle de l'abandon définitif de sa mère" (28). (In the boiling and pale light, the child still in her womb, she moves on, without fear. Her road, she is certain, is that of the definitive abandonment of her mother.) From her home on the plains of the Tonlé-Sap, a lake in present day Cambodia, the young woman wanders north, following an impossible itinerary through Cambodia and Thailand and over the Cardamome mountains, to India. Nearly starving along the way, her strength diminished by the fetus, she steals food and takes lovers to survive. She loses her hair and badly cuts her foot. When she imagines her mother's reaction upon seeing her return, she is paralyzed. Her mother's look freezes her in her steps, a maternal Medusa paralyzing her victim.

> Elle a peur. La mère fatiguée la regardera venir depuis la porte de la paillote. La fatigue dans le regard de sa mère: Encore en vie, toi que je croyais morte? La peur la plus forte, c'est celle-là, son air lorsqu'elle regardera s'avancer son enfant revenue. Tout un jour, elle hésite. Dans un abri de gardiens de buffles, sur la rive du lac, elle reste sous le regard, arrêtée. (26)

> She is afraid. The tired mother will see her returning from the door of the hut. Fatigue in the mother's look. "Still alive, you whom I believed dead?" The strongest fear is that one, her demeanor when she watches the daughter who has returned coming towards her. An entire day she hesitates. In a buffalo keeper's shelter, on the lakeshore, she remains beneath that look, frozen.

Paralyzed by a look, this daughter slowly goes mad. In her madness, she begins to inhabit her hallucinations. As if to escape the cruelty visited upon her, she imagines her sisters and brothers and a beneficent mother.

> Elle voit des frères et soeurs perchés sur une charrette, elle leur fait signe, ils rient eux aussi en la montrant du doigt, ils l'ont reconnue, elle se prosterne encore, reste, reste visage contre terre et se trouve devant une galette posée devant elle. Quelle main la lui aurait donnée sinon celle de sa mère? (27)

> She sees her brothers and sisters perched on a cart, she waves to them, they too laugh, pointing at her, they have recognized her, she prostrates herself again, remains, remains with her face against the ground and finds herself before a cracker placed in front of her. What hand would have given it to her if not her mother's?

The image of the prodigal's return and a caretaking mother fades and the young woman abandons in her turn, what has abandoned her. In a gesture recalling that of the heroine of *Hiroshima mon amour,* who declares her defiance by claiming to forget, the beggar-woman imagines another return home. She will be disdainful. "Ell reviendra pour lui dire, à cette ignorante qui l'a chassée: Je t'ai oubliée" (21). (She will return to tell her, to tell this stupid woman who drove her out, I have forgotten you.)

When her child is born, the young girl tries to give it away at the marketplaces that she haunts in the search for food. She beseeches other women to take her baby but they ignore or shun her, too poor to help or repulsed by her festering foot and apparent madness. She does not speak their language, but shows the infant in the hope that she will be understood. Eventually, a white woman takes the baby, at her daughter's insistence. They return to their home, trailed by the beggar-woman, mad now, who has completed her exile from Tonlé-Sap. Near the gates of the house from where she observes uncomprehending, a doctor arrives. The white woman is distressed, the child is dying, but the mother repeats only "Battambang" in singsong fashion, and laughs.[4] Relieved of its referential value, the name becomes mythical; the word becomes a song. The sonorous husk of the word alone remains like a corpse to attest to the past. Language become song signals the beggar-woman's madness; no record remains of the memory of her trauma, vaporized.

The beggar-woman is a typically Durasian heroine. She is a figure in which sexuality and maternity are conjugated with violence and death, memory and language abolished by madness. The musicality of language and of a musical rather than a signifying logic, what some have seen as the poetic orality of Duras's writing, is in the ascendancy at specific moments in Duras's texts.[5] These are moments of feminine madness or of definitive loss, as when the heroine of *Hiroshima mon amour* bids her lover farewell in a hypothetical future when their story would be "no more than a song." The cycle of maternal castigation and abandonment, madness and dispossession in an unjust social universe circulates through the texts of the Indian Cycle and is a recurrent theme in Duras's writing.

Like Jacques Hold, Peter Morgan is a narrator who writes a madwoman's story as a gesture of appropriation. With her pain he will be initiated into the pain of Calcutta. "Peter Morgan est un jeune homme qui désire prendre la douleur de Calcutta, s'y jeter, que ce soit fait, et que son ignorance cesse avec la douleur prise" (29). (Peter Morgan is a young man who wishes to partake of Calcutta's suffering, to throw himself into it, that it be done and that his ignorance cease with the possession of pain.) Hold revels in the suffering of the Indias, as he claims the others do. "Je m'exalte sur la douleur aux Indes. Nous le faisons tous plus ou moins, non? On ne peut parler de cette douleur que si on assure sa respiration en nous . . . Je prends des notes imaginaires sur cette femme. —Pourquoi elle? —Rien ne peut plus lui arriver la lèpre elle-même . . ." (157). ("I exalt in the suffering in the Indias. We all do more or less, don't we? We cannot speak of this suffering unless we are sure that it breathes in us. I am taking imaginary notes on this woman." "Why her?" "Because nothing more can happen to her, leprosy itself.") This framed narrative would be his initiation.

The beggar-woman is the perfect subject for Morgan. She embodies the suffering of India; her madness defines an end-point for suffering. She is someone to whom nothing more can happen. Moreover, she will never dispute Morgan's version of her biography for she no longer speaks. Her only language is the chant of her exile and madness, the single sound, Battambang. If Peter Morgan has free reign to represent her exile and madness, he must supply a language that she herself no longer possesses, and this language, like the imagination that Morgan must also employ, can be none other than his own. The act of narration, then, the male story of a madwoman's road to her madness, is less an enterprise of representation than one of pure fabrication and substitution. In the place of biography is the bios of the writer; the writer's desire shapes what has lost its form, resubjectifies the subjectless. "Peter Morgan voudrait maintenant substituer à la mémoire abolie de la mendiante le bric-à-brac de la sienne. Peter Morgan se trouverait, sans cela, à cours de paroles pour rendre compte de la folie de la mendiante de Calcutta" (73). (Peter Morgan would now like to substitute the bric-a-brac of his memory for her destroyed memory. Without this, Peter Morgan would find himself short of the words to describe the madness of the beggar woman of Calcutta.)

Typically, Duras places a male character in the role of a narrator who imposes a narrative form on a woman's abolished memory and paralyzed imagination. The female subject is absent from these biographies, which the male narrator misreads. Morgan does not write his story as an effort to cure the beggar-woman, as did Jacques Hold, nor to possess her in the sense that Lui tried to possess Elle, but to cure himself of his ignorance. And he will reiterate the abandonment of his subject, the abandonment with which Duras's narrators characteristically meet their own limits and which, here, echoes the mother's gesture. For if he can describe her filth, her excesses, her past, her trail of dead and abandoned children, he abuts the onset of her madness. "Je l'abandonnerai avant la folie, dit Peter Morgan, ça c'est sûr, mais j'ai quand même besoin de connaître cette folie" (183). (I will abandon her before madness, says Peter Morgan, that is certain, but I nonetheless need to know this madness.) Unlike Hold, Morgan refuses to be fascinated by his subject. He imposes a narration on the trauma of madness and suffering, which is not narrable. His fiction-making activity is a bald gesture. His language and his reason supplant that which has been destroyed.

Michael Richard, Stretter's lover, claims to understand Morgan's fiction and his narrative narcissism. "Je crois que ce qu'il [Richard] veut dire, dit Michael Richard, c'est plus encore, il voudrait ne lui donner d'existence que dans celui qui la regarderait vivre. Elle, elle ne ressent rien" (182). (I believe that what he means, says Michael Richard, is even more, he wants her to exist only in the person who would watch her live. She, she does not feel anything.) For Morgan, according to Hold, the insensible beggar-woman comes to life only insofar as a spectator sees her. "Elle serait à Calcutta comme un . . . point au bout d'une longue ligne, de faits sans signification différen-ciée? Il n'y aurait que . . . sommeils, faims, disparition des senti-ments, et aussi du lien entre la cause et l'effet?" (182). (In Calcutta, she would be something like a . . . point at the end of a long line, of events without any differentiated significance? There would only be . . . sleep, hunger, the disappearance of feelings, and also of the link between cause and effect?) If Morgan acknowledges his own limits and refuses to follow his heroine into her madness, Charles Rosset is less well able to sustain a distance between this mad siren and himself.

Charles Rossett pursues his own version of a rite of passage by facing head-on this cohabitant of sweltering Calcutta. He does so with fascination and horror. At the river where she washes herself and eats, he watches her. She plays to her audience, decapitates a live fish, and offers it to Rossett.[6] Like Morgan, who cannot tolerate the tale of the woman's madness, Rossett discovers that the sight of a woman's madness is more than he can bear. Veritable medusa. "La folie, je ne la supporte pas, c'est plus fort que moi, je ne peux pas . . . le regard des fous, je ne le supporte pas . . . tout mais la folie. . . ." (206). (Mad-ness, I cannot stand it, it is stronger than me, I cannot . . . the look of a madperson, I cannot stand it . . . everything but madness.) This feminine spectacle of madness horrifies and fascinates, intolerable spectacle of the madwoman.

If the first half of the novel focuses on the tale of the beggar-woman and finishes the story of her madness, the second half focuses on the co-star of the feminine constellation, Anne-Marie Stretter. Stretter and the beggar-woman are linked. They are said to share the secret of suffering. Stretter suffers. "Elle sait qu'ils sont là, tout près, sans doute, les hommes de Calcutta, elle ne bouge pas du tout, si elle le faisait . . . non . . . elle donne le sentiment d'être maintenant prisonnière d'une douleur trop ancienne pour être encore pleurée" (198). (She knows that they are there, near, without doubt, the men of Calcutta, she does not move at all, were she to . . . no . . . she gives the impression now of being a prisoner of suffering too old to cry about still.) Her acclimation to India has never been complete for when she traveled up the Mekong toward Savannakhet to meet M. Stretter near the Laotian border seventeen years ago, she fell ill. Her husband feared that she was unable to bear the suffering of India. It was during that trip that Stretter caught sight of a beggar-woman selling her child. She told this story to Morgan. This is their second link.

Music is the shared language of the feminine characters. Like the beggar-woman whose only language is her song, Stretter's Venetian dialect inflects her voice and overpowers the sense of what she says. "Charles Rosett perd le fil de ce qu'elle dit, il se met à l'entendre sans l'écouter—la voix, de cette façon, a des inflexions italiennes qu'il découvre" (191). (Charles Rosett loses the train of what she is saying, he begins to hear her without listening to her—her voice, in this fashion, has Italian intonations which he discovers.) Stretter was a musician, a talented pianist, the very hope of Venice. Her lover, Michael Richard, an English tourist in Calcutta, was on the verge of leaving India when he chanced to hear Stretter's piano playing from the street outside her residence. Soothed and intrigued, he listened for several evenings before entering the guarded house to meet her. Language and music are two poles, the one of signification and the other of passion, abolished memory, and suffering. The beggar-woman stands at one end of the spectrum; Stretter straddles the two.

Stretter and the beggar-woman are paired by their sexuality. Stretter is an easy woman who inflames the desire of those around her where the beggar-woman has been punished because of her extra-marital pregnancy. And typical of Duras's work, feminine sexuality is never evoked without some accompanying violence. Both characters incite real or imagined physical violence. With respect to Stretter, violence occurs at the level of taletelling, erupting systematically into the visual field. One example involving Charles Rossett situates the intersection between perception and fantasy at the periphery of sadism. This imagined scene carries the mark of fantasy, for it is imagined as perceived by Michael Richard.

L'image lui revient d'Anne-Marie Stretter droite sous le ventilateur—dans le ciel de ses larmes, dit le vice-consul, puis tout à coup l'autre image. Il voudrait l'avoir fait. Quoi? Qu'il voudrait, ah, avoir dressé sa main. . . . Sa main se dresse, retombe, commence à caresser le visage, les lèvres, doucement d'abord puis de plus en plus sèchement, puis de plus en plus fort, les dents sont offertes dans un rire disgracieux, pénible, le visage se met le plus possible à la portée de la main, il se met à sa disposition entière, elle se laisse faire, il crie en frappant: qu'elle ne pleure plus jamais, jamais, plus jamais; on dirait qu'elle commence à perdre la mémoire. . . . Michael Richard les regardait. (202).

The image of Anne-Marie Stretter erect beneath the fan comes back to him—in the heaven of her tears, says the vice-consul—then suddenly the other image. He would have wanted to do it. What? That he would have wanted, ah, to have raised his hand. His hand is raised, falls, begins to caress the face, the lips, softly at first then more and more briskly, then more and more strongly, the teeth are bared in an unflattering smile, painful, the face puts itself as much as possible within reach of the hand, it offers itself completely to him, she is passive, he yells while striking: that she never never cry again; she appears to begin to lose her memory. Michael Richard was watching them.

At the ambassadorial reception, Rossett again watches Stretter. The intensity of his gaze appears to immobilize her and Rossett imagines this initiate into the pain of India as dead. Vision or fantasy?

Il la regarde longuement, elle s'en aperçoit, s'étonne, se tait, mais il continue à la regarder jusqu'à la défaire, jusqu'à la voir assise à se taire avec les trous de ses yeux dans son cadavre au milieu de Venise, Venise de laquelle elle est partie et à laquelle elle est rendue, instruite de l'existence de la douleur. (191)

He looks at her for a long time, she becomes aware of it, is surprised, stops talking, but he continues to look at her to the point of undoing her, to the point of seeing her sitting, having stopped talking, with the cavities of her eyes in her cadaver in the middle of Venice, Venice from which she left and to which she returned, instructed in the existence of suffering.

Stretter, like the beggar-woman whose madness Rossett is unable to contemplate, generates a violent fantasy as she becomes the spectacular object of a male gaze. Anne-Marie Stretter. Aging but still strikingly beautiful, attentive to her two daughters, the elder of whom already resembles her, indulged by her husband and attended to by a coterie of indolent and properly dressed international bureaucrats and businessmen who gather around her at the French Embassy, she remains the mesmerizing center of the Indian Cycle. "Elle est plate, légère, elle a la rectitude simple d'une morte" (197). (She is flat, light, she has the simple rectitude of a corpse.) Stretter, siren of death.

The eponymous vice-consul of the novel is an unusual male character in Duras's universe. Like the beggar-woman, he is a figure of exclusion and incomprehension whose inability to adapt to the misery of India results in his eventual ostracism. Jean-Marc de H. is more properly the ex-vice-consul of Lahore. He has been removed from his post for having shot at lepers at night in the gardens of Shalimar. M. Stretter and his staff pore over his files hoping to find something in his dossier to explain his behavior. They find few details in his biography: educational successes, his parents' deaths, juvenile escapades, none provide insight into his actions in Lahore. Duras mocks the would-be psychologists in search of a larval state of madness and suggests, moreover, that biography is fundamentally a fiction with little power to illuminate and much less to cure.

Despite his momentary lapse, the vice-consul remains perfectly cordial and able to sustain polite conversations with other members of white Calcutta. Even if, as Morgan claims, white Calcutta would participate in the suffering of India, the character that has partaken of that suffering becomes as incomprehensible as the suffering itself. The Europeans cannot assimilate the vice-consul any more than the suffering of India, or the beggar woman's madness.

Like most of the other male characters, and despite the noteworthy absence of other feminine liaisons, Jean-Marc de H. conceives a special sympathy for Anne-Marie Stretter. He would be initiated into passion by her. This passion has no language. "Parce que j'ai l'impression que si j'essayais de vous dire ce que j'aimerais arriver à vous dire, tout s'en irait en poussière . . .—il tremble—, les mots pour vous dire, à vous, les mots . . . de moi . . . pour vous dire à vous, ils n'existent pas. Je me tromperais, j'emploierais ceux . . . pour dire autre chose . . . une chose arrivée à un autre" (125). (Because I have the impression that if I were to try to tell you what I would like to be able to say to you, everything would dissolve in dust . . .—he trembles—, the words to tell you, you, the words . . . from me . . . to tell you, you, the words do not exist. I would make a mistake, I would use words . . . to say something else . . . something which happened to someone else.) Exiled in this passion, mistrustful of language at the frontiers of passion, he will not be invited into Stretter's circle. Rather, she offers him a geographical metaphor of trauma. "Je crois qu'il faut que vous pensiez à une chose c'est que, parfois . . . une catastrophe peut éclater en un lieu très lointain de celui où elle aurait dû se produire . . . vous savez, ces explosions dans la terre qui font monter la mer à des centaines de kilomètres de l'endroit où elles se sont produites. . ." (129). (I believe that you must think of something, which is that sometimes . . . a catastrophe can explode at a great distance from the place where it should have exploded . . . you know, these explosions in the earth which make the sea rise up at several hundreds of kilometers from the place where the explosions happened.) The vice-consul responds to his rejection with a yell, a language of suffering that is not language.

Not surprisingly, the tale of two exiles finishes inconclusively. Typical of the Indian Cycle texts, the novel that recounts the mesmerizing power of the feminine and charts the inability of language to imagine its own limits opens into a visual form, a film. Just as Duras plays with the boundaries of narration, fiction, and fantasy, and with the borders of memory and language in *Le Vice-consul,* she complicates these relationships in *India Song* in terms proper to cinema; the new narrative regions she explores thwart traditional definitions of time and space.[7]

India Song

In a typically elliptical remark about the nature of the cinematic medium, Duras claims that the camera writes more completely than the pen.

En somme, oui, ça pose la question du cinéma, là, de l'image. On est toujours débordé par l'écrit, par le langage, quand on traduit en écrit, n'est-ce-pas; ce n'est pas possible de tout rendre, de rendre compte du tout. Alors que dans l'image vous écrivez tout à fait, tout l'espace filmé est écrit, c'est au centuple l'espace du livre. Mais je n'ai découvert ça qu'avec *La Femme du Gange,* pas avec les autre films.[8]

To sum up, yes, it raises the question of the cinema, there, of the image. One is always overwhelmed by writing, by language, when you translate into writing, right; it is not possible to render everything, to take everything into account. Whereas in the image you write completely, all of the filmed space is written. But I only realized that with *La Femme du Gange*, not with the other films.

Duras gives much attention here, and she is not the only one, to the image, the filmed space. For if *India Song* has attracted no small amount of interest in certain circles, it is in large measure due to the formal pyrotechnics of splitting sound and visuals. This technique was used already in *Hiroshima mon amour*. Later, Duras experimented on her own with the relationship between sight and sound in *La Femme du Gange*, the film that made *India Song* possible. "En réalité, *India Song* est consécutif de *La Femme du Gange*. Si *La Femme du Gange* n'avait pas été écrit, *India Song* ne l'aurait pas été."[9] (In fact, *India Song* follows *La Femme du Gange*. If *La Femme du Gange* hadn't been written, *India Song* would not have been.) Duras claims that the sound track is completely independent of the sounds and images in *La Femme du Gange,* and that she maintains this disjunction in *India Song.*

> *La Femme du Gange*, c'est deux films: le film de l'image et le film des voix, les deux films sont là, d'une totale autonomie, liés seulement, mais inexorablement, par une concomitance matérielle. . . . Les voix parlent dans le même lieu que celui du tournage du film de l'image, mais pas dans la partie de ce lieu retenu par la caméra. Elles se parlent. Elles ignorent la présence du spectateur. Il ne s'agit donc pas d'un commentaire. Ce ne sont pas non plus des voix off, dans l'acceptation habituelle du mot: elles ne facilitent pas le déroulement du film . . . elles l'entravent.[10]

> *La Femme du Gange* is two films, the film of the images and the film of the voices, the two are there, completely autonomous but tied together, inexorably, by a material concomitance. The voices speak in the same place in which the shooting occurs, but not in the same space where the camera focuses. They speak to each other. They ignore the presence of the spectator. It is therefore not a question of a commentary. These are not off voices, either, in the traditional sense of the word, they do not facilitate the film's unfolding, they create obstacles for it.

Are the visuals really independent of the sound track? There is some debate around this question and persuasive claims for a relationship of montage rather than radical disjunction.[11] And as we shall see, this question raises the other, familiar one, of images and narration. But before entering into that debate and exploring the film, it is important to clarify the terminology. What is a *voice off*, in the traditional meaning of the term? How and to what end does Duras pose her challenge? To answer requires some appreciation of the traditional relationship of sound to image from which Duras departs, that of classic narrative cinema.

ON AND OFF: SOUNDS AND IMAGES

On and off sound are defined in terms of the image.[12] The visibility or invisibility of the sound source at the moment of the sound's perception defines on and off, respectively. Light is projected through a dark space and reflected onto a flat screen where it is interpreted as a piece of a diegetic universe extending beyond the boundaries of the screen. Sound can support the illusion of a completely visible diegetic universe, and it can rupture it, making palpably clear that something is beyond vision, and may never be visible.[13] Sounds seem to come from some part of either the visible images (on) or the invisible (off) part of the diegesis. But on and off inadequately differentiates that category of sounds emanating from somewhere other than the diegetic universe.[14]

Michel Chion, one of the best writers on the subject, proposes three terms for describing the relationship of sound sources and images, hoping to account for sounds independent of the diegetic universe. These are off, off screen (hors champ) and in.[15] In the first two cases, the sound source is not visible. The source of off sound is located in another time and space (voice-over or movie music, for example) while an off screen sound source belongs to the diegesis but is temporarily out of sight. Chion calls off and off screen sounds acousmatic. He maintains the traditional definition of in—a sound whose source is visible on screen. Beyond clarifying the terminology, Chion explores the analogies between sound and image, and develops the notion of an aural equivalent of point of view, or point d'écoute. Not only does he ask "where do the sounds come from?" but also, "who listens?"[16] Who listens raises the question of identification. Where point of view provides a visual vehicle for spectatorial identification, the point d'écoute—hearing something that a character hears, or does not—aurally determines a spectator's identification. Chion's analogy between the processes of identification set in place by an image and sound is intriguing. But, he argues, the analogy between theoretical tools for describing images and sounds falters when it comes to the material supports. We can say that the screen is the place where we see the images, but how do we define the place of sound? Sounds come from the speakers which diffuse them, and give a variety of impressions of localization, depending on the technology of the sound system.

Sound has always been a troublesome element for this relatively new art form.[17] From its inception, cinema has been conceived of as a visual medium. The bias remains, even today, and is responsible, in part, for the relative theoretical inattention accorded the phenomenon of sound in the movies.[18] History and technology are one part of the picture; the camera could record images and a projector reproduce them before appropriate sound recording and reproducing instruments were developed. As of the late 1920s, sounds could be recorded and reproduced while the visuals were projected. When the technology was in place, sound changed the nature of the movies. Early filmmakers and theoreticians, in one of the most important polemics in the history of film, heatedly debated the consequences of allowing images to talk synchronously.[19] The argument raged around the status of the image and, consequently, around the nature of the art form itself. Including sound in a fundamentally visual medium would reduce it to little more than filmed theatre, some argued. Language would subjugate images that would thus be relegated to the status of illustrations. Dialogue would be in the ascendancy.

If sound changed the nature of the art form, synchronized sound changed the nature of cinematic realism. The simultaneity of a sound with the visibility of its source reinforces the illusion that the screen image is a real, complete world. Visibly moving lips and slamming doors, accompanied by audible voices and slamming sounds, better help the spectator penetrate the space of the fiction. The sound-space relationship is a crucial one in the creation of the cinematic illusion. Crucial as well for cinematic pleasure, without which a filmgoer would probably not pay good money to go to the movies.

Today's filmgoer is a sophisticated consumer of films, familiar with the technology by which images and sounds are recorded, edited, reconfigured and projected.[20] Notwithstanding his understanding of the operation of the illusion, the spectator willingly relinquishes critical distance to be absorbed by a film. Absorption is pleasurable, and accepting the three dimensionality of the world projected onto the flat screen is the first gesture toward it.[21] If pleasure is a motive for yielding to the filmic illusion, the vehicle is identification. Identification was recognized early on as a particularly powerful effect of this art form.[22] More than a simple identification between viewer and camera, several levels of identification between spectator and spectacle are possible.[23] The pleasure of spectatorial identification is complex.[24] The spectator identifies with the image and pleasure waxes. Complete absorption would be intolerable, however, for the film over, the illusion ended, where would the spectator be? Thus, displeasure and denial follow. The illusion is recognized as such and critical distance reestablished. For spectatorial pleasure to be preserved and jouissance held at bay, the illusion must be denied and the impression maintained that identification can be arrested by an act of will. The fiction can thus function and the pleasure of identification enjoyed and contained in the oscillation between spectatorial absorption and denial.[25]

That spectatorial pleasure arises from an illusory identification with an image has provoked some comparison with the mirror phase.[26] But, as Metz has pointed out, the screen is not a mirror and the spectator's body will never be reflected there. Cinematic identification has been decried by some as voyeurism. Feminists have noted that the image offered for visual consumption is often one of the female body. The spectator, regardless of gender, thus identifies the camera as a male gaze and identifies with this gaze. The complex processes at work of identification and denial at the cinema, and the pleasure of watching a scene unwatched, have linked the magic of the movies to the process of sexual differentiation.[27] Laura Mulvey has argued persuasively that the particular power of the cinematic image to induce spectatorial identification, and its strong form of fascination, inheres in its evocation or recapitulation of earlier, psychological structures.[28] Indeed, this is suggested elsewhere in Mannoni's elegant argument about the comic illusion.[29]

Classic narrative cinema possesses a number of techniques designed to preserve spectatorial identification undisturbed. The necessarily fragmentary diegetic universe—fragmented as much by the screen and camera as by sounds coming from off screen—is palliated by a number of shooting techniques. Nothing on screen accuses the spectator in his role as spectator. Shot-reverse shots suture the spaces of the diegesis. A travelling camera can similarly appear to aggregate the pieces of the diegetic universe. Deep focus, favored by Bazin because it allows the spectator to penetrate into the depth of the image and explore it, uses time as an ally in creating the illusion of a coherent, homogenous world even beyond the screen. The conventions of classic narrative cinema have established the norm.

Duras does not respect these conventions. She refuses to make narrative cinema. She uses sound and shooting techniques to confuse time and space rather than support any illusion of reality. The image-sound relationship disrupts the spatial and temporal signposts in the service of the illusion. The new narrative regions into which she casts her characters resists easy denomination by traditional narrative designations. The sounds of *India Song*, including more or less audible human voices in several languages, animals, rain, tides, and music, are a mixture of acousmatic and off. But they occupy an ambiguous space off, off screen, temporally elsewhere. Ambiguous, but not, as Duras claims, radically off and disjunctive. On more than one occasion, the images seem to be commented upon by the voices. The voices of visible characters seem to be audible on the sound track even if no lips move visibly. Despite her claim of independent sounds and images, Duras's images appear to fascinate the voices. The visual cues instruct us to understand the images as nostalgic rather than representational; where is this visible space located? From where and in what time frame do the voices speak? No synopsis or discussion of this film can ignore its formal pyrotechnics. These formal experiments notwithstanding, Duras's films alternately absorb and bore the spectator. She does not escape—and rather, invites—the spectatorial fascination inherent in this art form.

India Song has been described as a film in the nostalgic mode; the images are silent, the languorous and sole feminine center of male attention is treated like a Hollywood star, the cast is dressed in evening wear of the late 1930s.[30] Everything is calculated to enrapture. The cast of characters is penetrated by an odd air of distraction, the result of hearing the sound track played while the cameras were turning. This simple, material fact would argue for Duras's claim of an independent sound track. Separation is a technical reality, but the relationship of sound track and images creates a montage effect. To argue for a radical disjunction is to ignore that the images constitute a "foyer de fascination" for the spectator as well as for the voices on the sound track.

SYNOPSIS AND SEGMENTATION

Segmentations of this film rely on the sound track. The most scrupulously detailed of these divides *India Song* into prologue, story, and epilogue, according to the voice changes.[31] The prologue, dominated by women's voices, opens on a sun slowly setting over a green, rolling landscape. A female voice singing in Laotian laughs. Two young female voices begin a dialogue while the song's audibility fades. Off space is immediately stratified; the single voice and the couple's voices seem not to occupy the same space. The couple speaks about a beggar-woman from Savannakhet. Voice 1: "Une mendiante," and Voice 2: "Folle." They remember her story: Voice 2: "Ah! oui, je me souviens. Elle se tient au bord des fleuves. Elle vient de Birmanie." Voice 1: "Elle n'est pas indienne. Elle vient de Savannakhet. Née là-bas." ("A beggar-woman." "Mad." "Ah, yes, I recall. She keeps to the river banks. She comes from Birmanie." "She is not Indian. She comes from Savannakhet. Born there.") We take the singing and laughter suddenly to be those of the beggar-woman, relegated to an indeterminate past whose relationship with the voices is unclear. Is she audible to them? Remembered by them? The beggar-woman is linked to Anne-Marie Stretter and Calcutta. The two voices recount their story in the past tense. "A Calcutta, elles étaient ensemble," Voice 1 says. "La Blanche et l'autre?" ("In Calcutta they were together." "The white woman and the other one?") The immobile camera continues to frame the setting sun. The sounds change and a piano plays a song that becomes the theme. What is the source of the piano music? Is it off or off screen? Does it occupy the same space or time as the voices or the beggar-woman? Again, off space thickens as the piano music marks a shift in images. In an interior shot, a turbaned servant places flowers next to a photo of a young woman (one of at least three photos by Boubard shown atop the piano). The immobile camera frames the piano and flowers, and incense slowly wafts through the still image. We follow the servant in the mirror as he retreats and exits into reflected contiguous space, rear left into the penumber, his path marked by the lit candle he carries. The somber image prepares us for the announcement that Stretter is dead and the piano and photo take on the significance of an altar. A slow, close-up pan of a dress, jewels, and wig follows. The voices recall Lol and the ball and recall, as well, that Stretter ravished Lol of her lover.

V1:   Michael Richardson était fiancé à une jeune fille de S. Tahla, Lola Valérie Stein. . . .
V2: Le mariage devait avoir lieu à l'automne. Puis il y a eu ce bal . . . ce bal de S. Tahla.
V1: Elle était arrivée tard à ce bal . . . au milieu de la nuit . . . habillée de noir. . . .
V2: Que d'amour ce bal, que de désir. . . .

V1: Michael Richardson was engaged to a young girl from S. Tahla, Lola Valérie Stein. . . .
V2: The marriage was supposed to take place in the fall. Then there was this ball . . . this ball of Tahla.
V1: She came to the ball late . . . in the middle of the night . . . dressed in black. . . .
V2: Such love this ball, such desire. . . .

The voices comment on the light, the monsoon, the dust, and the smell of leprosy in Calcutta. "Où est-on?" ("Where are we?") asks Voice 2. Excellent and appropriate question posed in the present tense and to which the image seems to respond. A scaling château comes on screen. A voice intones. "L'Ambassade de France aux Indes." The camera penetrates (into what is, in fact, another château) and a voice asks: "De quoi avez-vous peur?" a pan left stops on a photo of a young woman. Stretter's name is pronounced. How else to understand the image than as one of Stretter? "Morte là-bas aux îles. Trouvée morte." ("Dead there, in the islands. Found dead.") Simple sentences follow. The voices shift to a past tense, and then, in a characteristically Durasian move, to the present tense. "Ils dansaient." "Ils dansent." ("They were dancing." "They are dancing.") In counterpoint, the image shifts. A male character, back to a mirror, watches a couple, reflected in a mirror, dancing. Stretter? Despite the photo, despite the announcement of her death, the images incarnate the name. Inevitably Stretter. The couple stops. All three characters slowly leave the room. In a long shot, we see a sole male character. The name of the vice consul is pronounced. Virtually the entire cast of characters from *Le Vice-consul* has appeared or been named in this prologue. The voices's reference to Lol Stein broadens the time frame and geography of the novel.

Loud music opens the second part of the film, the story. Dance tunes seem to emanate from the space of the visuals. "Avant, il y a eu ce bal." ("Before, there was this ball.") The story concerns the ambassadorial reception at which the vice consul will make his desire known to Stretter and she will dance with her various admirers. The feminine voices of the prologue remain audible. A number of new voices (including those of the actors on screen and Duras herself) become audible. Occasional sentence fragments stand out clearly against more muffled background voices. The theme song and rhumba (by Carlo Alessio) as well as Beethoven's Diabelli Variations are audible at well-paced intervals.

The transition from the story to the epilogue is not as aurally evident as that from prologue to story. A very long shot (almost six minutes) of five immobile characters opens the third part of the film, and the voices tell us that we are in the islands. Stretter and her coterie plus one sojourn at the Prince of Wales Hotel. A light intensifies, dims, and intensifies again as the voices speak in the present tense. "Ici" punctuates their conversation as if they were cohabitants of in space. The news of Stretter's suicide concludes the epilogue. In the final shots we see Stretter alone in a darkened room. She rises and exits through French doors rear left, her red hair haloed by the light. After the voices have spoken of the lovers's pact of a double suicide, they recount her drowning, and the subsequent discovery of her peignoir, found washed ashore. The final shots pan a French map of Indochina while the beggar-woman's song and laugh are again audible.

The space of the film, like the space and temporality of the voices, is stratified. On and off screen together occupy the screen thanks to mirrors. For example, in Shot 7 the camera focuses on a clock atop a mirrored mantle. The mirror reflects a second off-screen mirror obliquely, whose reflection we see. An infinite regression of chandeliers appears in this contiguous, virtual space. Duras projects her characters into this new narrative region, illusory, repetitive and insistently imaginary.

The interplay of voice and image challenge traditional narrative. Not because they are radically separate, but because they are ambiguously linked. The voices seem to converge on the images, drawn to them. As if demonstrating the lesson of *Le Ravissement de Lol V. Stein*, the female voices of the prologue are contaminated by their storytelling. Fascinated, they reiterate the mortal passions of the ball whose drama they intone. When Voice 1 asks: "Sur quoi pleurez-vous?" Voice 2 answers: "Je vous aime jusqu'à ne plus voir, ne plus

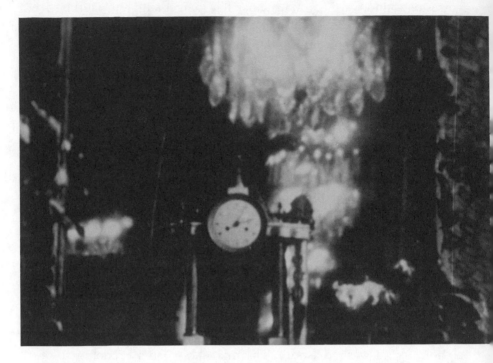

Shot 7

entendre, mourir." (1: "What are you crying about?" 2: "I love you
to the point of blindness, deafness, death.") Narrator or player in the
drama? Narrative frontiers are blurred.

Numerous examples of the sound-image relationship suggest that
rather than rupture, there is, as Ropars insists, montage between
sound track and images. "De quoi avez-vous peur?" is answered with
a shot of a photograph and the name, "Anne-Marie Stretter." Characters at the reception dance in time to the music. Similarly, and also at
the reception, we see Stretter and Rossett and Stretter and the vice-
consul. Lips unmoving, the characters seem nonetheless to be speaking because we hear a conversation between them. The montage is
persuasive. So too is the image of the vice-consul's departure and his
audible screams. Verb tenses, adverbs, voice changes, counterpoint of
question and (visual) answer, souvenirs serving as narrative commentary, all these strongly suggest a montage of image and sound track.
The difficulty of the temporal relationships between images and

voices or sounds, however, remains. The images suggest that they are reflections of a past, but how past with respect to the sounds? The voices are audible but their relative temporality stratifies off screen space and time and skews, at moments, the temporality of on screen images. The desire of the voices to wrest the story from the past inflects the film with a palpable nostalgia.[32] The melancholic mode and peculiar space of the on and reflected images, the stratified temporality of the voices, the immobile camera, all these constitute an arsenal in the service of non-narrative, non-representational cinema. Taken together with the delectation in framing, this use of image and sound reflects a fantasmatic activity. At its center, the disruptive and fascinating character of Anne-Marie Stretter.

> *Fantasme* . . . scénario imaginaire où le sujet est présent et qui figure, de façon plus ou moins déformé par les processus défensifs, l'accomplissement d'un désir inconscient.[33]

> Fantasy . . . an imagined scene in which the subject is present and in which an unconscious desire, more or less transfigured by the defenses, is realized.

> La fascination du récit fantasmatique . . . le récit-cadre celui qui, comme le cinématographe, change sans cesse de point de vue . . . rend impossible la localisation de l'énonciation: qui voit, qui regarde?[34]

> The fascination of a fantasmatic tale . . . the story-frame that, like the cinematographer, ceaselessly changes point of view . . . rendering the localization of the enunciation impossible: who speaks? who is looking?

MIRRORED SPACE

At the center of the Indian Cycle and often literally at the center of the images in *India Song*, Anne-Marie Stretter exerts a powerful visual fascination. At the same time, she figures a resistance to narrative representation. Object and figure of a properly fantasmatic structure at once within the diegesis and for Duras herself, Stretter is a character of excessive powers.[35] The following stills suggest that the mirrored space in which Stretter's image is doubled, introduces into the already illusionistic space of the frame, an off screen, adjacent space that is visible and visibly a fiction. Often framed in the mirror

Shot 9

or in doorways or by other characters, Stretter draws characters and camera toward her, organizes gazes and disrupts spatial frontiers. She arrests movement, but explodes representation.[36]

A photograph elicits the name Stretter. We see Delphine Seyrig, well-known star of French cinema. Seyrig becomes Stretter. First appearing in shot 9 dancing with Michael Richardson, she and her partner are observed by a spectator leaning against the mirror, his back to his reflection. We understand that he is watching the couple dance before him even if they are reflected behind him in the mirror. Its edge is discernible to the spectator's left. Anne-Marie Stretter stands between the two men, the object of gazes (the camera's, the spectator's, the film spectator's). But what is the status of this scene? Where is the couple? In contiguous, reflected off screen space or in a space imagined by the spectator? Are they remembered? By whom? From whose point of view is this shot organized? The status of the image with its double frames of screen and mirror, recalls that of the ball scene in *Le Ravissement de Lol V. Stein;* unattributable, indistinguishably fantasy or fiction, an insistent scene that figures itself, a scene in which a spectator, unobserved, is observed observing.[37]

Shot 69 is a variant of Shot 9. Stretter appears on screen with another male character while Michael Richardson sits to the right in the same space, his back to a small mirror. The mirror obliquely reflects some piece of the space to the left of the couple. Richardson sits on the ledge, framed by the embrasure, looking away from the couple. At the center of the image, Anne-Marie Stretter sutures on and off. She looks at the other man who embraces her, both reflected and beheld by Richardson. Our gaze is relayed by his as, immobile, he looks ahead, apparently into the contiguous space whose reflection we see on. The complexity of the image, the relay of gazes, and the multiplicity of frames are set in motion by Stretter.

Shot 69

Shot 18 is a veritable explosion of spaces and frames. The camera, posed at a slight oblique to the mirror, reflects the room with the piano in which entries and exits proliferate. It is only when Stretter, dressed in a black peignoir, traverses the image from off screen that we understand that we are watching reflected space. This is a peculiar space, contiguous to and extending on space, it is both on and elsewhere. Stretter's space. She moves in front of the mirror laterally while penetrating the deep space reflected in the mirror at the center of the frame. These spacial ambiguities trouble temporal correlatives. Stretter's reflection precedes her entry; when she enters the frame, the shot is reassessed. Stretter plays with frames, eluding and multiplying them, disrupting clear spatial and temporal boundaries, confusing point of view, making its localization impossible.

Shot 18 (1)

Shot 18 (2)

Shot 18 (3)

Shot 18 (4)

When we see Shot 39, we hear characters speaking without seeing their lips move. Stretter stands obliquely to a mirror, her reflection at the center of the image, between her and the male character. Stretter is doubled, reflected, she occupies an ambiguous space. The dance scene that follows pays tribute to the fantasy of the ball. The couple observed by the spectator, observed by the mirror, inhabits an illusionistic space dislocated by its multiplication. Like the multiplication of Lol's fantasy, this scene figures an internal duplication. The mirror deepens space and Duras projects the dance into that fantasmatic and fascinating territory of illusory, elusory repetition.

Shot 39 (1)

Shot 39 (2)

Over ten minutes long, Shot 52 is one of the longest and most elaborate of the mirror shots. It beautifully demonstrates the seduction of illusionistic space and the derealization of "real" characters. Stretter has entered from the right and is looking to the right. Only when we see her enter the space do we comprehend that we have been watching her advance from off to on space; her reflection, mistaken for her presence, is now doubled by it. As she turns, she averts her gaze and stands obliquely, shoulder left, to the mirror. She will continue to turn her back to the camera into the mirror as she watches the vice-consul approach.

The drama unfolds in the mirror (frame 1). We watch as Stretter watches as the vice-consul advances toward her reflection (4). The distance between them is never closed. Stretter retreats to a deeper space than that of the vice-consul (6), but not before the reflection has opened up an impossible space of encounter. Playing reflection against "real," making off screen on screen and conjoining it with an on that looks into the reflected off become on, multiplying reflections and exposing their seductive illusionism of the mirror, Duras demonstrates the disruptive fascination of Stretter. The character figures the gaze, fascinates the spectator by engaging him in a fantasmatic activity that is properly Duras's own.

Shot 52 (1)

Shot 52 (2)

Shot 52 (3)

Shot 52 (4)

Shot 52 (5)

Shot 52 (6)

FASCINATION AND FANTASY: FROM OEUVRE TO BIOGRAPHY

No other shibboleth is so often used to describe the effect of Duras's works on readers and filmgoers as the term *fascination.* Fascination is a theme and an effect with a performative dimension in Duras's texts. Characters are fascinated and fascinate each other, reader and spectator are similarly absorbed. Can this radicalized moment of an identificatory process lay bare an earlier and fundamental structuring moment of the subject? Isn't this fascination the measure of the fantasy text?

The Indian Cycle characters are fascinated and fascinating. Lol Stein, fascinated by Stretter who takes her lover and her place, is entirely dispossessed. For Lol, fascination is to be taken in the strongest sense, a question of identity, of the life and death of the subject. The beggar-woman, like Lol, is dispossessed by a mother figure, and her biographer is stopped in his tale by her horrifying madness. Unlike Lol's biographer this narrator is not enraptured. The beggar-woman evokes Stretter, the element of suture and the figuration of fascinating fantasy in the Indian Cycle.

Fantasy is a subject's interrogation of his or her biography.[38] Duras's fascination with Stretter begins in Indochina where Stretter, a woman she sees but never meets, becomes an idealized alternative to a mad mother. The image is fissured but Stretter remains a fascinating figure for Duras. Observed through the lens of Duras's biographical fascination, the Indian Cycle becomes a thematic and formal experimentation with the content and structure of fantasy as scene and text.[39]

4
Autographies and Fictions

"[J]e me demande si les autres femmes de mes livres ne l'ont pas masquée longtemps, si derrière Lol V. Stein il n'y avait pas Anne-Marie Stretter, parce qu'il n'y a pas de raison. Cette fascination dure toujours, je ne m'en sors pas, c'est une véritable histoire d'amour. . . . Quelquefois je me dis que j'ai écrit à cause d'elle."[1]

"D'où vient la fascination qu'elle exerce? C'est à vous autres de le dire, je ne sais pas."[2]

(I wonder if the other women in my books have not hidden her for a long time, if Anne-Marie Stretter was not behind Lol. V. Stein, because there is no reason that this fascination should still exist, I cannot free myself from it, it's a veritable love story. . . . Sometimes I say to myself that I wrote because of her.

From where does the fascination which she exercises come? It is up to you others to say, I do not know.)

Or, qu'est-ce que la fascination, si ce n'est pour ainsi dire la forme tempérée ou clémente du sentiment d'étrangeté ou d'incroyable familiarité *(Unheimlichkeit)* qui surgit quand il y a en face de moi (ou dans ce qu'il y a en face de moi dans le *Gegenstand*) quelque chose d'ignoré mais qui est cependant la racine de mon identité, qui m'est à moi-même étrangère?[3]

(But what is fascination, if not the tempered or clement form of a feeling of strangeness or of incredible familiarity [*unheimlichkeit*] which surges forth when there is, before me [or in the object before me, *gegenstand*] something which is unknown yet at the root of my identity and which remains foreign to me.)

THE MEMORY, THE FANTASY

Anne-Marie Stretter[4] is both a key to the Indian Cycle and to Duras's familial and social universes, in which her oeuvre is anchored.[5] Throughout the Indian Cycle and in many interviews touching on her childhood, Duras designates Stretter as an enduringly fascinating figure who stands out starkly against the ground of Duras's past. Stretter, the veiled and feminine engine of numbers of Duras's texts exerts a fascination that Duras invites others to interpret. Her fascination is a measure of the pulverizing impact of Duras's family romance on her imagination and fiction, and a clear obstacle to any easy delimitation of the boundaries between the fictional, the fantasmatic, and the real in her autobiographical texts.[6]

Duras was born in French Indochina in 1914. She spent her childhood in different towns in contemporary Vietnam, along the Mekong, as well as in Saigon and Cambodia.[7] She grew up speaking Vietnamese and, apparently to her own surprise, was apprised by her mother that she was French and a member of the white race.[8] Her mother was a schoolteacher from Picardy, in the north of France. She and her husband had moved to the colonies to better their lot but her husband fell ill, returned to France, and died soon thereafter. Duras was four and the youngest of the three children. She, the younger of her two brothers and their mother remained in Indochina where poverty, corruption, and a daily spectacle of senseless suffering indelibly left their mark, one rendered often in her Indian Cycle texts as a cry, an inarticulate protestation of the pain provoked by the cruel order of things.[9]

The mother's relatively poor financial situation was exacerbated by her unwise investment. With her savings of twenty years, she purchased a piece of land on which she hoped to cultivate rice. Naively unaware that land-registry agents had to bribed if one was to receive a good parcel, she unwittingly took possession of uncultivable terrain, inundated by the sea during six months of the year. The dikes she built against the tides (not of the Pacific but of the China Sea) in the hope of reclaiming the land were destroyed. Ruined and enraged at the injustice she suffered, she became an intermittent mother, periodically depressed.[10] The story of the dikes, which she incessantly recounted, became her children's lullaby.[11] The pathos of her situation is announced in *Un Barrage contre le Pacifique:*

> Et qui n'aurait été sensible, saisi d'une grande détresse et d'une grande colère, en effet, à l'image de ces barrages amoureusement édifiés par des centaines de paysans de la plaine enfin réveillés de leur torpeur millénaire par une espérance soudaine et folle et qui, en une nuit s'étaient écroulés comme un château de cartes, spectaculairement, en une seule nuit, sous

l'assaut élémentaire et implacable des vagues du Pacifique? Et qui, négligeant d'étudier la genèse d'une si folle espérance, n'aurait été tenté de tout expliquer, depuis la misère toujours égale de la plaine jusqu'aux crises de la mère, par l'événement de cette nuit fatale et de s'en tenir à l'explication sommaire, mais séduisante du cataclysme naturel? (24)

Who indeed would not have been overwhelmed with anger and distress at the thought of those dykes, lovingly built by hundreds of peasants suddenly awakened from a thousand years of torpor by a wild hope—those dykes which had spectacularly collapsed like a house of cards in a single night, under the elemental, implacable assault of the Pacific? Would not anyone who had omitted to study the genesis of so crazy a hope have been tempted to explain everything, from the monotonous wretchedness of the plain to the mother's seizures, by the happenings of that fatal night? (20)[12]

Duras is less simply sympathetic than this narrator. She does not speak easily either about her mother or about her childhood. "J'avais dix-huit ans quand je suis partie [d'Indochine] pour passer ma philo ici . . . et faire l'Université et je n'ai plus pensé à l'enfance. Ç'avait été trop douloureux. J'ai complètement occulté"[13] (I was eighteen when I left to go to France for my last year of high school and to go to the University. I stopped thinking about my childhood. It had been too painful. I completely repressed it.)

Stretter belongs to the world of Duras's childhood, but that privileged part of it enjoyed by the French colonial administration in Indochina, a world from which Duras was excluded. Stretter's was the cushioned universe that Duras associates with tennis courts and black limousines.[14] The central and elusive figure in the cast of characters and on the landscapes of the Indian Cycle is remembered above all else as a "donneuse de mort."[15] Duras was between seven and eleven years old when she first saw the pale red-head in Vinhlong, on the Mekong.[16]

MD: Je ne sais même pas si ce n'était pas son vrai nom, Stretter, je ne crois pas l'avoir inventé ce nom. Ou bien je l'ai déformé, voyez, ou bien c'était ce nom-là, Stretter. C'était une femme rousse, je me souviens, qui ne se fardait pas, qui était très pâle, très blanche, et qui avait deux petites filles. Jamais je ne lui ai parlé. C'est loin, je ne sais plus très bien, je la voyais passer le soir dans son automobile avec son chauffeur. Avec la fraîcheur, elle sortait.[17]

I do not even know if Stretter was her real name, I do not believe that I invented it, this name. Or I deformed it, you see, or else it was that name,

Stretter. She was a very pale, very fair red-head, I remember, who did not wear makeup and who had two young daughters. I never spoke to her. It was long ago, I no longer really know, I saw her go at night in her car with her chauffeur. With the evening coolness, she went out.

Duras idealizes Stretter as a model parent.

Je me demande si l'amour que j'ai d'elle n'a pas toujours existé. Si le modèle parental ça n'a pas été elle, la mère de ces deux petites filles, Anne-Marie Stretter, non pas ma mère, voyez, que je trouvais trop folle, trop exubérante, et qui l'était d'ailleurs.[18]
On pourrait dire que cette femme, Anne-Marie Stretter, très longtemps, avait eu une fonction maternelle à mon endroit, une fonction parentale aussi importante que celle de ma mère.[19]

I wonder if the love that I have for her hasn't always existed. If the parental model was not her, this mother of two little girls, Anne-Marie Stretter, not my mother, you see, whom I found too crazy, too excitable and who, moreover, really was.
You could say that this woman, Anne-Marie Stretter, for a long time, had had a maternal function for me, a parental function as important as my mother's.

As important as her mother's? Her status is that of an alternative; Stretter palliates the horror of Duras's excessive and intermittently depressed mother about whom she does not speak easily.

[J]e retrouve un certain état dans lequel ma mère tombait parfois et dont déjà . . . nous connaissions les signes avant-coureurs, cette façon, justement, qu'elle avait, tout à coup, de ne plus pouvoir nous laver, de ne plus nous habiller, et parfois même de ne plus nous nourrir. Ce grand découragement à vivre, ma mère le traversait chaque jour. Parfois il durait, parfois il disparassait avec la nuit. (*L'Amant*, 22)

I rediscover a certain state into which my mother sometimes lapsed and of which, already . . . we recognized the precursor signs, this manner, precisely, which she had, suddenly, of being no longer able to wash us, no longer [able to] dress us, and even sometimes of no longer feeding us. This immense discouragement in living, my mother lived it daily. Sometimes it lasted, sometimes it disappeared with the night.

For despite Duras's sympathy for her mother's tragedy and her admiration for her excessive passion, her filial love is complicated by the feelings attendant upon her mother's illness. Hatred.

Dans les histoires de mes livres qui se rapportent à mon enfance, je ne sais plus tout à coup ce que j'ai évité de dire, ce que j'ai dit, je crois, avoir dit l'amour que l'on portait à notre mère mais je ne sais pas si j'ai dit la haine qu'on lui portait aussi et l'amour qu'on se portait les uns les autres, et la haine aussi, terrible, dans cette histoire commune de ruine et de mort qui était celle de cette famille dans tous les cas, dans celui de l'amour comme dans celui de la haine. (*L'Amant*, 34)

In the plots of my books which have to do with my childhood, I suddenly no longer know what I avoided saying, what I said, I believe I have described the love which we felt for our mother but I do not know if I acknowledged the hatred which we felt for her also and the love we felt for each other, and the hatred also, tremendous hatred, in this shared history of ruin and death which was that of this family in all cases, in the case of love as well as in that of the death.

Humiliation and a fury born of it. Inattentive to what she wore, Duras's mother embarrassed Duras when she arrived, ill-dressed, to pick her up from school in a jalopy. "Tous les enfants ont honte de leur mère quand elle est mal-habillée, les cheveux tirés. . . ."[20] (All children are ashamed of their mother when she is badly dressed, hair pulled back.)

[S]es souliers, ses souliers sont éculés, elle marche de travers, avec un mal de chien, ses cheveux sont tirés serrés dans un chignon de Chinoise, elle nous fait honte, elle me fait honte dans la rue devant le lycée, quand elle arrive dans sa B.12 devant le lycée tout le monde regarde, elle, elle s'aperçoit de rien, jamais, elle est à enfermer, à battre, à tuer. (*L'Amant*, 32)

[H]er shoes, her shoes are worn, she does not walk correctly, she has a lot of difficulty, her hair is pulled back and drawn into a bun, like a Chinese woman, she makes us ashamed, she makes me ashamed in the street in front of the high school, when she comes in her B.12 in front of the high school everyone looks, she, she does not notice anything, never, she should be locked up, beaten, killed.

Frustrated anger and bewilderment at this partial mother who preferred her first child. "C'était son enfant. Je ne sais pas comment des injustices de cet ordre puissent s'installer puisqu'en principe, la mère aime de façon également préférentielle tous ses enfants."[23] (He was her child. I do not know how such injustices can settle in, because ideally, mothers love each of their children with equal preference.) Not only her preference for her first child, but her complicity with him in the death of her youngest. "[J]e suis hantée par la mise à mort de mon frère. Pour la mort, une seule complice, ma mère" (26). (I am haunted by the execution of my brother. For his death, a single accomplice, my mother.) Duras takes leave of her mother at the death of this younger, beloved brother.

> Le petit frère est mort en trois jours d'une broncho-pneumonie, le coeur n'a pas tenu. C'est à ce moment-là que j'ai quitté ma mère. C'était pendant l'occupation japonaise. Tout s'est terminé ce jour-là. Je ne lui ai plus jamais posé de questions sur notre enfance, sur elle. De même que mon frère aîné. Je n'ai pas surmonté l'horreur qu'ils m'ont inspiré tout à coup. Ils ne m'importent plus. Je ne sais plus rien d'eux après ce jour. (*L'Amant*, 37)

> The little brother died in three days from bronchial pneumonia, his heart gave out. It is at that moment that I took leave of my mother. It was during the Japanese occupation. Everything ended that day. I never again asked her any questions about our childhood, about her. The same for my older brother. I have not overcome the horror with which they suddenly inspired me. They are no longer important to me. I know nothing about them after that day.

Duras's profoundly conflicting remarks about her mother display all the pathos of a child's love besieged by an unbearable melancholy, a child's love for an absent parent absorbed in private passions and illness. "J'ai eu ce paradis de cette mère qui était tout à la fois le malheur, l'amour, l'injustice, l'horreur."[22] (I had this paradise of this mother who was at one and the same time misery, love, injustice, and revulsion.) Stretter, on the other hand is perceived as elegant, orderly, and equitable, a perfect mother in contrast to the one who is indifferent to her appearance, emotionally chaotic and unjust. Stretter becomes a model for Duras, yet a model whose status varies. Duras appears to be unable to accept her at one and the same time as a parental, maternal, and feminine model. As if each ideal can only supplant the other, as if each feminine incarnation must displace the other.

> Je pense que c'était ça, elle, Anne-Marie Stretter, le modèle parental pour moi, le modèle maternel, ou plutôt le modèle féminin; elle ne m'apparaissait pas comme maternelle, elle était avant tout une femme adultère, voyez, non pas la mère des petites filles.[23]

> I think that that was it, she, Anne-Marie Stretter, the parental model for me, the maternal model, or rather, the feminine model; she did not seem maternal to me, she was, above all else an adulteress woman, you see, not the mother of those little girls.

The impossible conjugation of the maternal and the sexual, stems, arguably, from the unassimilability for Duras, of the two. We can infer at least some serious obstacle to their peaceful cohabitation from Duras's reaction to the news that a young man had killed himself when Stretter left with her husband.[24] Her stupefaction is disproportionate to the news, particularly given that she never met Stretter but only espied her. The conjugation of a maternal ideal and feminine sexuality explodes because of the suicide, according to Duras, the death of a young man.

C'est peu après son arrivée qu'on a appris qu'un jeune homme s'était suicidé par amour pour elle. Je me souviens du bouleversement que ça a provoqué en moi, je ne comprenais plus rien. Le choc, qui a été très fort, quand j'ai appris cette nouvelle venait du fait que cette femme n'était pas apparemment une femme coquette, une femme mondaine; elle avait quelque chose d'invisible, c'était le contraire d'une femme qui se remarque, elle était très silencieuse, on ne lui connaissait pas d'amis et elle se promenait toujours seule ou bien avec ses deux petites filles comme dans le livre, Le Vice-consul. Et puis, tout d'un coup on a appris cette nouvelle. Si vous voulez, elle a incarné pour moi longtemps une sorte de double pouvoir, un pouvoir de mort et un pouvoir quotidien. Elle élevait des enfants, elle était la femme de l'administrateur général, elle jouait au tennis, elle recevait, elle se promenait, etc. Et puis elle recelait en elle ce pouvoir de mort, de prodiguer la mort, de la provoquer.[25]

It was not long after her arrival that we learned that a young man had killed himself for love of her. I remember that I was overwhelmed by this news, suddenly, nothing made sense to me. The shock, which was very great when I learned this news, arose from the fact that there was nothing apparently either coquettish or mondain about this woman; she had something which was not visible, she was the opposite of a woman you would notice, she was very quiet, was not known to have any friends and she always walked alone or with her two little girls like in Le Vice-consul. And suddenly, we learned this news. If you will, she has long incarnated for me, a sort of double power, the power of death and an ordinary, daily power. She raised her children, she was the wife of the head administrator, she played tennis and entertained, she took walks, etc. And she concealed within herself this mortal power, this ability to provoke and promulgate death.

That the news of Stretter's past provokes so profound a shock compels certain readers to wonder how much Duras invented, and really remembered, and what the real shock is.[26] The term *primal scene*, which Duras uses to refer to these memories, gives some indication of the explosive conjugation. The disturbing revelation that the figure who veils the mad parent unveils her own sexuality rocks the already unstable ground of the maternal.

> En tout cas, c'est comme la scène primitive dont parle Freud. C'est peut-être ma scène primitive, le jour où j'ai appris la mort du jeune homme. Tu sais, c'était une mère, sage, raisonnable, et ces deux petites filles toujours en blanc, c'était ses enfants, et cet homme, ce mari, était un père—moi je n'avais pas eu de père, et ma mère vivait comme une nonne—c'était la mère des petites filles qui avaient mon âge qui possédait ce corps doué de pouvoir de mort. Il y avait des réceptions, tout ça était très régulier, en ordre, le tennis, le parc, le Mékong, les sorties, le tour d'inspection chaque soir, le cercle européen, si triste, au bord du Mékong. . . . Tout d'un coup, dans cette espèce d'univers parfait et pour moi, comment dirai-je, immobilisé—l'accident—l'accident: le suicide par amour de cette femme—le jeune homme qui se tue pour elle. . . . Pour que ça m'ait fait un choc tel, tu comprends, je me dis que ça devait me concerner, que ça réapparaisse quarante, cinquante ans après, c'est que ça devait me concerner de très, très près.[27]

> At any rate, it is like the primal scene of which Freud speaks. Perhaps it is my primal scene, the day I learned about the death of the young man. You know, she was a mother, well-behaved, sensible, and her two little girls always in white, these were her children, and this man, this husband was a father—me, I had not had a father and my mother lived like a nun—it was the mother of little girls who were my age, who had this body that had the power of death. There were receptions, all that was very normal, as it should be, the tennis courts, the park, the Mekong, the outings, the evening inspection, the European circle, so sad, along the banks of the Mekong. . . . Suddenly, in this sort of perfect universe, and for me, how shall I say, immobilized, the accident, the accident—the suicide for love of this woman—the young man who kills himself for her. For that to have been such a shock, you understand, I tell myself that it must have had something to do with me, to have it reappear forty, fifty years later, it must have been something that concerned me very, very intimately.

To call this already exaggerated reaction a primal scene is a curious choice of terms; there is neither a scene nor any overt sexuality in this account. In fact, Duras sees nothing; the illusion-shattering news comes her way through the local grape vine; it is a dialogue and not an image that makes of Stretter a *donneuse de mort*.[28] Duras's constant comparison between Stretter and her mother suggests that both have a Medusa-like impact of paralysis and death. For the spectacle of the mother's tragedy has similarly petrified not only her daughter, but her entire family, and has introduced a ruptured visual circuit.

C'est une famille en pierre, pétrifiée dans une épaisseur sans accès aucun. Chaque jour nous essayons de nous tuer, de tuer. Non seulement on ne se parle pas mais on ne se regarde pas. Du moment qu'on est vu, on ne peut pas regarder. . . . Nous sommes ensemble dans une honte de principe d'avoir à vivre la vie. C'est là que nous sommes au plus profond de notre histoire commune, celle d'être tous les trois des enfants de cette personne de bonne foi, notre mère, que la société a assassiné. Nous sommes du côté de cette société qui a réduit ma mère au désespoir. A cause de ce qu'on a fait à notre mère si aimable, si confiante, nous haïssons la vie, nous nous haïssons. (*L'Amant*, 69)

It is a family of stone, deeply petrified and unattainable. Each day we try to kill ourselves, to kill. Not only do we not speak to each other, but we do not look at each other. As soon as you are seen, you cannot look. . . . We are together in a shame of principle for having to live life. It is there that we are at the deepest reach of our common history, that of being all three of us the children of this person of good faith, our mother, whom society has assassinated. We are on the side of this society that has reduced my mother to despair. Because of what they did to our mother, so lovable, so trusting, we hate life, we hate each other.

Pieces of this complex web of associations linking a maternal figure with madness and death and sexuality take on, at different moments, more and less prominence in Duras's writing. The suicide of a young man becomes the leitmotiv in Duras's memories; each mention is part of a larger picture interweaving intolerable and omnipresent associations between Stretter, death, desire, and the maternal figure. Stretter is a focal point and blind spot for Duras, occulting fantasies by becoming the anchor for others turning around the maternal figure so present in two of Duras's autobiographical works, *Un Barrage contre le Pacifique* and *L'Amant*. Neither of these texts constitutes an official autobiography. Both are partial, dwelling on the powerful passions in which Duras was enmeshed as an adolescent in Indochina. *L'Amant* comes after the family is dead. Written during four months in the country, it is the unavowed center of a drama published almost forty years earlier.

UN BARRAGE CONTRE LE PACIFIQUE

Un Barrage contre le Pacifique, the novelistic version of her mother's ruin in Indochina, radically censors Duras's first love affair. Duras tempers her style in order to keep the novel harmonious for the sake of her readers.[29] For the sake of her mother's equanimity, Duras reveals neither her liaison with a man not of her race nor her sexual passion.[30]

A mother and her two children, Suzanne, seventeen, and Joseph, twenty lead a monotonous life on the coastal plain where they live in a dilapidated bungalow.[31] Their mother's efforts to make the land cultivable by building a sea wall against the Pacific have failed; she is outraged by bureaucratic corruption and nature itself. The children are restless and each looks for some change. Joseph, adored by both his mother and sister, hunts in the jungle and trysts with different women. Suzanne, still a virgin at the novel's outset, hopes that a traveler will take a detour from the main road and carry her off.

The mother's ruin and despair are a backdrop against which her children's love affairs unfold. Each of these, as well as the mother's renunciation of sexual liaisons, is connected with the cinema. When she is dying, Joseph recounts her story to Suzanne, a gesture with which he takes leave of his mother and offers a legacy to his sister.

Il ne croyait plus qu'elle pourrait vivre encore très longtemps mais contrairement à autrefois il croyait que ça n'avait plus beaucoup d'importance. Lorsque quelqu'un avait tellement envie de mourir on ne devait pas l'en empêcher. Tant qu'il saurait la mère vivante il ne pourrait d'ailleurs rien faire de bon dans la vie, rien entreprendre. Chaque fois qu'il avait fait l'amour avec cette femme, il avait pensé à elle, il s'était souvenu qu'elle, elle n'avait jamais fait l'amour depuis que leur père était mort parce qu'elle croyait, comme une imbécile, qu'elle n'en avait pas le droit, pour qu'ils puissent eux, le faire un jour. Il lui raconta qu'elle avait été très amoureuse d'un employé de l'Eden pendant deux ans, c'était elle qui le lui avait dit, et qu'elle n'avait jamais couché avec lui une seule fois toujours à cause d'eux. Il lui parla de l'Eden. De l'horreur qu'étaient ces dix ans que la mère avait passés à tenir le piano à l'Eden. Il s'en souvenait mieux qu'elle parce qu'il était plus grand. Et elle-même lui en avait quelquefois parlé. . . . La mère jouait pendant deux heures. Il lui était impossible de suivre le film sur l'écran: le piano était non seulement sur le même plan que l'écran mais bien au-dessous du niveau de la salle. En dix ans la mère n'avait pas pu voir un seul film. . . . (243–45)

He no longer believed that she could live very much longer. But now this no longer seemed so important as he had once thought. When someone wanted to die as much as all that, you ought not to stop them. Moreover, as long as he knew the mother was still alive, he would never be able to make good in life, never start up anything on his own. Every time he had made love to this woman, he had thought about the mother. He remembered that she had never made love to anyone since their father died because she thought, idiotically, that she had no right to, for their sakes.

He told Suzanne that she had been very much in love for two whole years
with a man who worked at the Eden and that she had never slept with
him, not even once, because of the two of them. He talked to her about
the Eden, about the horrors of those ten years the mother had spent
playing the piano there. He remembered better than Suzanne because he
was older and because the mother herself had sometimes talked to him
about them. . . . The mother played for two solid hours. It was impossible for her to follow the film on the screen: the piano was well below the
level of the auditorium. (201–2)[32]

At a silent cinema, the mother provides the musical accompani-
ment. Playing the piano in the orchestra pit, she is materially prevented from seeing the screen. It is here, in this false eden of silent
films where visual pleasure is frustrated and where music and images
are separated, that she abstains from sexual pleasure. For her children,
however, the cinema is a place to which they go with pleasure. For
both, the cinema is a fantasy space explicitly linked with sexual
adventure. The space can be understood both as the physical theater
in which they take refuge, and as the cinematic fiction with which
they identify. But if the cinema offers the children a refuge where it
provided none for their mother, their fantasies are dissimilar. Joseph
meets the woman who will free him from his mother's reins at the
cinema.

J'étatis allé au cinéma, dit Joseph à Suzanne. Je m'étais dit, je vais aller au
cinéma pour chercher une femme. . . . Et quand les lumières s'éteig-
naient, que l'écran s'éclairait et que tout le monde la fermait, alors j'étais
comme autrefois, je n'attendais plus rien, j'étais bien. . . . C'est au cinéma
que je l'ai rencontrée. (221–22)

Depuis trois ans, il attendait qu'une femme à la détermination silencieuse
vienne l'enlever à la mère. Elle était là. (260).

"I had gone to the cinema," said Joseph to Suzanne. "I'd said to myself,
I'm going to the cinema to find a woman. . . . And when the lights went
out and the screen lit up [and everyone shut up], then I felt just the same
as I used to. I wasn't waiting for anything any more. . . . I was perfectly
all right. . . . It was at the cinema that I met *her.* (183)

For three years he had been waiting for a woman of that silent determina-
tion to come and carry him away from the mother. Now she was there.
(213)

For Suzanne, however, the fantasy serves another purpose. Initially, she goes to the Eden cinema, like Joseph, seeking refuge. Refuge from the city, from her mother, and from her assiduous and ridiculed Chinese suitor, M. Jo. Unlike Joseph, however, she does not retreat to the cinema in search of her sexual fantasies. Willfully naive perhaps, she refuses to understand her friend's remark that going to the movies serves as a sexual preinitiation. "Avant de faire l'amour vraiment, on le fait d'abord au cinéma. . . . Le grand mérite du cinéma c'était d'en donner envie. . . ." (172). (Before really making love, you begin at the cinema. The great merit of the cinema was that it made boys and girls want to. . . .) (143) For Suzanne, the cool darkness of the movie hall offers a purgative, healing solace.

> C'était l'oasis, la salle noire de l'après-midi, la nuit des solitaires, la nuit artificielle et démocratique, la grande nuit . . . plus vraie que la vraie nuit, plus ravissante, . . . plus consolante . . . choisie, ouverte . . . généreuse . . . dispensatrice, la nuit où se consolent toutes les hontes, où vont se perdre tous les désespoirs, et où se lave toute la jeunesse de l'affreuse crasse d'adolescence. (163)

> It was the oasis, the darkened room of the afternoon; the artificial, democratic night of the lonely; the great equalizing night of the cinema. More real than the real night, more enchanting and consoling than any real night, it was open to all and offered to all . . . generously. It was the night which comforted all shame and dissolved all despair; the night in which youth could wash away the appalling filth of adolescence. (136–37)

Snugly seated in the comforting darkness, Suzanne watches a royal heroine find her prince. When the camera moves in for a close-up of their first kiss, the audience is absorbed. "Gigantesque communion de la salle et de l'écran. On voudrait bien être à leur place. Ah! comme on le voudrait" (164). (There is an immense communion between the audience and the screen. Everyone longs passionately to be in their place) (136). Who is this "on"? What narrator is this who claims such desire for the audience? And where is this desired and desiring place? It is the characters' place with which the audience identifies that makes the images mesmerizing.[33] But at the moment when Suzanne forgets that the film is a fiction and identifies with the characters, at the moment when she relinquishes the safety net of the denial of the image's reality, the love scene is brutally transformed.[34] When the scene threatens to serve as Suzanne's sexual initiation, sexuality becomes a threat. Her identification with the characters—or with the camera—constitutes a transgression of the maternal example of sexual abstinence and produces a nightmare: the close-up of a kiss becomes a violent severing of body and head, a grisly slow-motion act of cannibalism.

Leurs bouches s'approchent, avec la lenteur du cauchemar. Une fois qu'elles sont proches à se toucher, on les mutile de leurs corps. Alors, dans leurs têtes de décapités, on voit ce qu'on ne saurait voir, leurs lèvres les unes en face des autres s'entrouvrir, s'entrouvrir encore, leurs mâchoires se défaire comme dans la mort et dans un relâchement brusque et fatal des têtes, leurs lèvres se joindre comme des poulpes, s'écraser, essayer dans un délire d'affamés de manger, de se faire disparaître jusqu'à l'absorption réciproque et totale. Idéal impossible, absurde auquel la conformation des organes ne se prêtent évidemment pas. Les spectateurs n'auront vu pourtant que la tentative . . . [c]ar l'écran s'éclaire et devient d'un blanc de linceul. (164)

[T]heir mouths come nearer and nearer, with the slowness of a nightmare. The moment they are about to touch, they are mutilated of their bodies. Then one sees their lips slowly opening wider and wider in their disembodied heads. Their jaws drop like those of corpses until, suddenly, the heads relax and the lips fasten upon each other like octopuses. They are crushed against each other in a frenzy of hunger, as if each mouth were seeking to devour and totally annihilate the other. Impossible, absurd ideal for which the lips were so obviously not designed! But all the spectators see is the frantic attempt . . . [f]or, suddenly, the screen is lit up and becomes as white as a shroud. (136–37)

Who authors the abrupt and brutal fantasy? Duras's narrator seems to adopt Suzanne's point of view; the fantasy is Suzanne's. Appearing suddenly, the nightmarish scene is quickly shrouded by the white screen. The traumatic spectacle and mutilated bodies warn this daughter of an abstemious mother against erotic impulses. The "place" of sexual desire and of sexual intimacy is one that she must not occupy. The fantasy of corporeal absorption and death, which burst onto the screen in a momentary projection of unconscious fears, is effective. Suzanne will not make love at the movies. The cinematic fantasy space reveals and defends against visual pleasure.[35]

Suzanne is not without reason to fear her mother's reaction to her sexual desires. When wrongly accused of sleeping with M. Jo, a suitor the family humiliates constantly, Suzanne is beaten by her mother. Screaming abuses at her daughter, the mother castigates her as a prostitute. "[J]'en ai marre, marre d'avoir des enfants comme j'en ai. Une saleté de fille comme j'ai là" (116). (I'm fed up, fed up with having children like mine. With such a slut of a daughter as I have . . ." (97). Duras describes a spectacle of independent image and sound in this violent scene. As the mother beats the silent Suzanne, she narrates another tale: her troubles, the sea wall, her ruin, and her outrage. Joseph watches in silence before intervening in favor of his sister. Referring to her in the third person, the voice so often reserved for the Durasian heroine, he protests. "Merde, tu le sais bien qu'elle a pas couché avec lui, je comprends pas pourquoi tu insistes. —Et si je veux la tuer? si ça me plaît de la tuer?" (118) (Hell, you know perfectly well she hasn't slept with him. I can't think why you keep nagging her. Suppose I want to kill her? Suppose it would give me pleasure to kill her?) (99).

The question is rhetorical, but no less serious for being so. For if Suzanne is the object of her mother's wrath, directed as much against the daughter's pleasure as against the possibility of her affair with a Chinese man, she is also the object of her murderous pleasure. Maternal pleasure would deprive the daughter of her own voice, her own pleasure, and of her own self. The mother's desire defines Suzanne as a subject of deadened sexual desire or, more radically, as a dead subject.

When Suzanne leaves the Eden cinema, distressed by the nightmare she has imagined, she searches for Joseph with a new urgency. "Elle se remit à chercher Joseph mais pour d'autres raisons que tout à l'heure, parce qu'elle ne pouvait se résoudre à rentrer. Et aussi parce que jamais encore elle n'avait eu un tel désir de rencontrer Joseph" (164). (She began once more to look for Joseph but this time for another reason, because she could not make up her mind to go back to the hotel. And, also, because, never before, had she felt such a longing to meet Joseph) (137).

Where the cinema buries Suzanne's sexual fantasies, it only reconfirms her passion for her brother. Even M. Jo had noticed early on that "Suzanne, elle n'avait d'yeux que pour ce frère . . ." (39). (Suzanne had eyes only for this brother . . .) (32). Like her mother, Suzanne adores her brother and when she decides to take a lover, she chooses Jean Agosti, a local companion and friend of Joseph whose father runs the canteen in Ram. Agosti, who had kissed her a year prior while *Ramona*, a favorite tune of Joseph, was playing, reminds her of her brother. "Une fois, à la cantine de Ram, pendant qu'on jouait *Ramona*, ils s'étaient embrassés. On aurait peut-être pu dire qu'il ressemblait à Joseph" (276). (Once, at the canteen in Ram, while they were playing *Ramona,* they had kissed each other. In some ways, he was not unlike Joseph) (226). Agosti's laugh and voice as well remind Suzanne of her brother. "Il se mit à rire un peu sourdement comme quelquefois Joseph" (289). (He gave a rather hollow laugh as Joseph sometimes did) (236). "Sa voix aussi rappelait celle de Joseph" (293) (His voice too reminded her of Joseph's) (238).

If Suzanne enjoys her sexual initiation with Agosti and becomes his lover while her mother is dying, her belief that she will always love her brother more than any other man remains unshaken. "Suzanne se souvenait parfaitement de cette minute où elle sut qu'elle ne rencontrerait peut-être jamais un homme qui lui plairait autant que Joseph" (267–68). (Suzanne vividly remembered that moment in which she had realized that she would never meet another man who would attract her as much as Joseph) (219). "Quand il réfléchissait comme ce soir . . . on ne pouvait pas s'empêcher de le trouver très beau, de l'aimer très fort" (124). (When he sat thinking, as he did tonight, thinking with difficulty and distaste, she could not help finding him very handsome and loving him very much) (105). At the end of the novel, Suzanne chooses to remain with her brother and his lover; the familial triangle is preserved when the three leave the miserable plain on which the mother is buried.

The cinema fantasy passage in this novel links sexuality with violence and death just as certainly as they are linked in Duras's account of her memories about Stretter and the young man who killed himself for her. The link provokes a trauma that effectively arrests the fantasy of desire. If a visual image is a charged arena of desire for Duras, narration would serve to contain and defuse the desire. The temporal dimension of this relation between narration and visual images establishes another tension, that between the timelessness of images and the progressive temporality of narrative. What is more, these Durasian tensions point to a fundamentally impossible representation of feminine sexuality. For if Duras's oeuvre is, if nothing else, one that cries pleasure, this pleasure is announced, reiterated, and mourned as having been fleetingly and intensely present before being killed off.

PASSIONS

The character Suzanne's passion for her brother evokes Duras's passion for her brother, the Joseph of the novel, the brother whom

Duras's mother did not prefer.[36] Duras wanted to protect this *petit frère* two years her elder, against their eldest brother whose cruelty and status of preferred child provokes a murderous and maternal expression of sororal love.

> Je voulais tuer, mon frère aîné, je voulais le tuer, arriver à avoir raison de lui une fois, une seule fois et le voir mourir. C'était pour enlever de devant ma mère l'object de son amour, ce fils, la punir de l'aimer si fort, si mal, et surtout pour sauver mon petit frère, je le croyais aussi, mon petit frère, mon enfant, de la vie vivante de ce frère aîné posée au-dessus de la sienne, de ce voile noir sur le jour, de cette loi représentée par lui, un être humain, ce qui était une loi animale, et qui à chaque instant de chaque jour de la vie de ce petit frère faisait la peur dans cette vie, peur qui une fois a atteint son coeur et l'a fait mourir. (*L'Amant*, 13–14)

> I wanted to kill, my older brother, I wanted to kill him, to be able for once to get the better of him, just once, and to see him die. It was in order to remove from my mother the object of her love, this son, to punish her for loving him so much, so badly, and most of all to save my little brother, I also believed this, my little brother, my child, from the living life of this older brother poised above his, from this black veil against the day, this law represented by him, decreed by him, a human being, and which was an animal law, and who, at each moment of each day in the life of this young brother, was the terror of his life, a terror that on one occasion reached his heart and killed him.

When he died, Duras suffered as if for the loss of a lover, a child, herself.

> Le petit frère. Mort. D'abord c'est inintelligible et puis, brusquement, de partout, du fond du monde, la douleur arrive, elle m'a recouverte, elle m'a emportée, je ne reconnaissais rien, je n'ai plus existé sauf la douleur, laquelle, je ne savais pas laquelle, si c'était celle d'avoir perdu un enfant quelques mois plus tôt qui revenait ou si c'était une nouvelle douleur. Maintenant je crois que c'était une nouvelle douleur, mon enfant mort à la naissance je ne l'avais jamais connu et j'avais pas voulu me tuer comme là je voulais. (*L'Amant*, 127)

> The younger brother. Dead. At first, it was incomprehensible and then, suddenly, from everywhere, from the depths of the world, pain arrives, it enfolded me, it carried me, I recognized nothing, I no longer existed except as pain, which, I did not know which, if it was the return of the pain of having lost a child a few months earlier or if it was a new pain. Now I believe that it was a new pain, my child, dead at birth, I had never known him and I had not wanted to kill myself as then I did.

Duras's reaction to the news of her brother's death recalls her reaction to the news of Stretter's suitor's death: a paralysis so intense that it threatens her own existence. A paralysis that circulates throughout Duras's texts. With the news of her brother's death, an illumination. She grasps, suddenly, the intensity of her love. Extreme. The loss, intolerable, provokes a desire for her own death.

On m'a télégraphié. J'ai voulu mourir. Je me souviens qu'on m'empêchait de mourir. Je me jettais contre les murs. Je voulais me casser la tête contre les murs. Je ne pouvais absolument pas tolérer la mort de ce jeune frère, absolument pas. Puis j'ai pensé souvent après à ça, je me suis dit "quand même c'est étrange de souffrir à ce point là, à ce point là de la mort d'un frère." Puis j'ai découvert, j'ai découvert, oui, tardivement, que je l'avais sans doute aimé, plus que tout.[37]

They sent me a telegram [to Paris]. I wanted to die. I remember that they stopped me from dying. I threw myself against the walls. I wanted to break my head against the walls. I was absolutely unable to bear the death of this young brother, absolutely unable. Then I often thought about it after that, I said to myself, "still, it is strange to suffer so, to suffer so because of a brother's death." Then I discovered, yes, late, that I had doubtless loved him more than anything.

Duras draws an explicit comparison between her adored brother and the Chinese lover whom she did not avow in *Un Barrage contre le Pacifique.* "Il y a quelque chose en lui qui est du petit frère, du fait de la race. Pour mon petit frère du fait qu'il était en retard, ils se rejoignent."[38] (There was something about him of the younger brother, because of his race. For my brother, it is the fact that he was slow that brings them together.) It is not simply their alterity, but the passion with which Duras loves them both that confounds the two. Both desired and loved with an intensity perceived only at the moment of their loss. For Duras, the epiphany involves another punctual male suicide. When asked whether or not she loved her first lover, Duras hesitates before answering.[39] She was eighteen, aboard a steamer bound for France when she realized that she had loved him intensely. "[S]ur le bac qui me ramenait en France, un jeune homme s'est tué. Cette séparation du corps du jeune homme m'a rendu à cette évidence que je l'avais aimé. C'est cette séparation d'avec le corps du jeune homme mort qui m'a rendu à cette évidence là, je l'ai sans doute aimé." (On the boat returning me to France, a young man killed himself. This separation from the body of the young man forced me to accept the evidence that I had loved him. It is this separation from the body of the young dead man that forced me to accept that evidence that I doubtless loved him.) It is this passion, along with those other long-seething incestuous passions, that constitutes the center of *l'Amant*, and of which Duras says, "Et à partir de *[L'Amant]* j'ai compris combien je désirais mes frères, surtout le petit." (And ever since *[L'Amant]* I have understood how much I desired my brothers, especially the younger one.)

L'Amant

"L'Histoire de ma vie n'existe pas." (p. 14)

Un Barrage contre le Pacifique is autobiographical and censored. It is a traditional novel, respectful of the canons of realism and of familial obligations. Like this early work, *L'Amant* recounts Duras's familial universe in Indochina.

> J'ai beaucoup écrit de ces gens de ma famille, mais tandis que je le faisais ils vivaient encore, la mère et les frères, et j'ai écrit autour d'eux, autour de ces choses sans aller jusqu'à elles. . . . Avant, j'ai parlé des périodes claires, et de celles qui étaient éclairées. Ici je parle des périodes cachées de cette même jeunesse, de certains enfouissements que j'aurais opérés sur certains faits, sur certains sentiments, sur certains évenéments. (*L'Amant*, 14)

> I have written a lot about these people in my family, but while I did so they were still alive, the mother and the brothers, and I wrote around them, around those things without going right up to them. . . . What I am doing here is different and the same. Before, I spoke of the clear periods, of those which have been illuminated. Here I speak about the hidden periods of this same youth, of certain burials that I would have imposed on certain facts, certain feelings, certain events.

Duras is free to write about her family after the deaths of her mother and two brothers. If *L'Amant* is a family epitaph, it is no less an interment of familial passions and rages that produces a catharsis which her heroines rarely enjoy. "Je pense que c'est ça, *L'Amant*. J'ai innocenté tout le monde. . . . Depuis que j'ai raconté en toute liberté, c'était fini, le ressentiment terrible que j'avais contre [mon frère aîné.]³⁸ (I believe that that's *L'Amant*. I disculpated everyone. Ever since I freely told the story, it was over, the terrible resentment which I had against [my older brother].) *L'Amant* acknowledges the loss of passions which, in their living, prohibited their telling.

Ils sont morts maintenant, la mère et les deux frères. Pour les souvenirs aussi c'est trop tard. Maintenant je ne les aime plus. Je ne sais plus si je les ai aimés. Je les ai quittés. Je n'ai plus dans ma tête le parfum de sa peau ni dans mes yeux la couleur de ses yeux. Je ne me souviens plus de la voix, sauf parfois de celle de la douceur avec la fatigue du soir. Le rire, je ne l'entends plus, ni le rire, ni les cris. C'est fini, je ne me souviens plus. C'est pourquoi j'en écris si facile d'elle maintenant, si long, si étiré elle est devenue écriture courante. (38)

They are dead now, the mother and the two brothers. For the memories also, it is too late. Now I no longer love them. I no longer know if I loved them. I have left them. I no longer have the perfume of her skin in my mind, nor in my eyes the color of her eyes. I no longer remember the voice, except sometimes the voice of gentleness, with the fatigue of evening. The laugh, I no longer hear it, neither the laugh nor the cries. It is finished, I no longer remember. This is why I write about her so easily now, at such length, so extensively, it has become fluent writing.

In the opening passage, Duras takes leave of her family. She begins on a barge traversing the Mekong, and the final stage will be on another boat departing Southeast Asia for France, where she will have a sudden illumination of what has been lost. *L'Amant* records these moments. But if this is an epitaph of traumatic loves and losses, it is not a tale fully husked of emotions. Duras can write because she is unbound from her family, while her lover who eclipsed all the others in her life remains an unnamed and shadowy figure whose chief role is to be a purveyor of intense, inconsolable sexual pleasure.³⁹

In its form, *L'Amant* resembles a running commentary on a family album.⁴⁰ Duras invites her readers to look with her. "Vous voyez," she says. The photos produce neither melancholia nor nostalgia; all that has been swept away. The style is recognizable. There is the familiar repetition and limited vocabulary, the slow, rhythmic adumbration of nouns that accumulate to impart a density to the vision. This structure, with its interweaving perspectives of first and third persons, and visual mosaics, creates a fugal pattern. Linear temporality is jettisoned while the setting of the major events is altogether specific: Colonial Indochina in the late 1920s, Saigon and its Chinese quarter of Cholen, the two and one half years of Duras's affair. The limited cast of characters appears and reappears in altered poses. Abruptly and without transition, Duras describes the principals; now her lover, now her mother, now her brother. The apartment in Cholen where her lover takes Duras, the high school in Saigon and rooms where she boards, the family bungalow and parcel, these are the sites between which the narrative and black limousine wend their way.

There are other, minor figures. The innocently beautiful schoolhood friend, Hélène Lagonelle, who inspired Duras with intense desire. And, in the only real leap beyond Indochina, occasional references to women in wartime Paris. And there is Stretter and the beggar-woman. Fragments, scenes, images, sounds, memories are touched upon and expanded, circulate and return within this curious photo album. The freedom to write about her first love affair clearly does not entirely eviscerate the fascination of certain memories.

The text begins with a pre-text. "Un jour, j'étais âgée déjà. . . ." One day a man told her that he prefered the face she has today, dévasté, un visage détruit, she calls it, to the beautiful one she wore as a young girl. This is the image that Duras alone contemplates, "toujours là dans le même silence, émerveillante. C'est entre toutes celle qui me plaît de moi-même, celle où je me reconnais où je m'enchante." ([A]lways there in the same silence, astonishing. Of all the images of myself, this one pleases me the most, the one in which I recognize myself, in which I charm myself.) Enraptured Duras ravishes her readers, demanding that they observe her fascination as she beholds the self she recognizes, herself having been—"se regarde avoir été.[41] There is a coquetry in this pose that recalls Duras's delectation of isolated, immobile images. The familiar tension between narrative temporality and the atemporality of fascinating images is apparent here as well. Over and again Duras refers to her memories, as well as to particular photos ("[L]a photo du désespoir. Celle de la cour de la maison de Hanoi" [41]. "L'image commence bien avant qu'il ait abordé l'enfant blanche près du bastingage . . ." [45]. "L'image de la femme aux bas reprisés a traversé la chambre" [50].) as images which, narrated, display all the intensity of their present-tenseness. There is no life history here. How could there be when the gaze is thus self-absorbed and immobile?

As if to confirm the striking visualness of her memory, Duras tells us that *L'Amant* was to have been called *La Photographie absolue* for a photo that was never taken. This was a photo of Duras crossing the Mekong. Casting herself as something of a Helen, she is an adolescent proud of what she has understood to be her powers of seduction. The face at the origin of this story is the one she wore at fifteen and a half, on which all could read "de la jouissance et je ne connaissais pas la jouissance" (pleasure and I did not know pleasure) (15).

The portrait becomes an establishing shot. Duras on a ferry crossing the Mekong, dressed provocatively in her mother's hand-me-down worn silk sheath, high-heeled lamé pumps and, incongruous detail, a man's hat. When she first tried it on, Duras tells us, and looked at herself in a mirror, the reflection became an image detached from her. "Soudain je me vois comme une autre, comme une autre serait vue, au-dehors, mise à la disposition de tous, mise à la disposition de tous les regards, mise dans la circulation des villes, des routes, du désir" (20). (Suddenly I see myself as an other, as an other would be seen, from outside, put at the disposition of all, put at the disposition of all gazes, put into the circulation of the cities, the roads, of desire.) This fundamental relationship with herself as with a self-image perceived and detached dominates the structure of this work. There is no accusation here against the necessary transformation by the process of writing of the self. It is inevitable.

When the commentary swerves back to the barge on the Mekong, there is the black car in which "un homme très élégant me regarde" (a very elegant man watches me) (25). It is not until seventeen pages later, following Duras's account of her announced intention to write, opposed by a mother who wanted her to complete her studies in math despite her admiration of such complete certainty about professional life, that Duras describes the total permeation of her life by this mother. Indeed, the lover's story is told in the third person and described in the present tense. "L'homme élégant est descendu de la limousine, il fume une cigarette anglaise. Il regarde la jeune fille au feutre d'homme et aux chaussures d'or. Il vient vers elle lentement. . . . Elle le regarde. Elle lui demande qui il est" (42–43). (The elegant man got out of his limousine, he is smoking an English cigarette. He looks at the young girl with the man's felt hat and golden shoes. He comes toward her slowly. . . . She watches him. She asks him who he is.) The photo begins before he approaches the white girl. She knows him, she claims, knows that he is afraid and that she is forever taking leave of her family by accepting his offer. A sense of destiny infuses the memory become present but at the same time, the third-person voice allows Duras to contemplate herself.

It is not until several days later that the affair will be consummated. He takes her to his studio apartment and here, "Elle est sans sentiment très défini, sans haine, sans répugnance non plus, alors est-ce sans doute là déjà du désir" (47). (She is without any very definite feeling, without hate, without repugnance either, thus is it without doubt there already, desire.) Duras discovers desire as if by a process of elimination. Desire is not these other feelings. Yet even as he initiates her into an intense pleasure confirming the promise of her face, Duras describes a detachment. A real detachment? A literary feint punishing the lover for his forced rejection of her? Impossible to discern. She asks him to be with her as he is with other women, not to talk to her. Crying, overcome by the rejection, he moves to the other side of the bed. She reacts, eyes closed, by drawing him closer, undressing him. Her discovery of his skin, indescribably soft, sensual, his sex golden, sumptuously smooth, body weak, he is afraid, always afraid, his hands are perfect, he despairs at the future of his love for her, understands that his father will forbid their marriage, that she will leave him, that she will never love him. Her desire grows as his mournful lament continues, her pleasure always intense and her orgasm incomparable.

There are two curious aspects of the accounts of Duras's lovemaking with her lover. One is her detachment. The other is her envisioned solution, which is to orchestrate a triangle by imagining her friend Hélène Lagonelle. A friend whose beauty inspires Duras with explicit and intense desire. "Je suis exténuée du desir d'Hélène Lagonelle. Je suis exténuée de désir" (92). With Hélène L., Duras would construct a relay for her pleasure. A voyeurist fantasy, to be sure, reminiscent of the visual triangulation of desire in *Le Ravissement de Lol. V. Stein.*

Je veux emmener avec moi Hélène Lagonelle, là où chaque soir, les yeux clos, je me fais donner la jouissance qui fait crier. Je voudrais donner Hélène Lagonelle à cet homme qui fait ça sur moi pour qu'il le fasse à son tour sur elle. Ceci en ma présence, qu'elle le fasse selon mon désir, qu'elle se donne là où moi je me donne. Ce serait par le détour du corps de Hélène Lagonelle, par la traversée de son corps que la jouissance m'arriverait de lui, alors définitive.
De quoi en mourir. (92)

I want to bring Hélène Lagonelle with me, there where each evening, eyes closed, I have myself given this pleasure which makes me cry out. I would want to give Hélène Lagonelle to this man who does that on me so that he does it in turn on her. This in my presence, that she do it according to my desires, that she gives herself there where I give myself. It would be by the detour of her body that the pleasure would find me from him, thus definitive.
To die from.

Duras appears to intensify her own desires and pleasure by the interposition of another woman, unless the other woman is her mother. She speaks to her lover about her beloved mother, her madness, and her exploitation; she speaks of a mother whose death is near. "Que la mort très proche de ma mère doit être aussi en corrélation avec ce qui m'est arrivé aujourd'hui" (51). (The proximate death of my mother must also be related to what happened to me today.) Maternal interdiction thus make its inevitable appearance in this room in Cholen. Like Joseph who could not make love without thinking of his mother until after her death. Here the mother's image is one of contrast, confirming Duras's difference and eventual departure from the family. "La mère n'a pas connu la jouissance" (50). (The mother did not know orgasm.) Thus, Duras shifts to the first-person, reflecting upon her ability to detach herself from her mother's interdiction. "Je me demande comment j'ai eu la force d'aller à l'encontre de l'interdit posé par ma mère" (50–51). (I wonder how I had the strength to go against the interdiction established by my mother.) The links between pleasure, mother, and death, are fundamental for Duras. Oscillation in narrative voice is in some measure that between identification and difference.

When she asks her daughter about the motive of the liaison Duras claims never to have avowed, the mother declares their difference, as if acknowledging what she is supposed not to know and confirming her daughter's self-enfranchisement. "Elle dit: je ne te ressemblais pas, j'ai eu plus de mal que toi pour les études et moi j'étais sérieuse, je l'ai été trop longtemps, trop tard, j'ai perdu le goût de mon plaisir" (114). (She says, I wasn't like you, I had more difficulty than you at school and I was serious, I was serious for too long, too late, I have lost the taste of my pleasure.) If the mother declares their difference gently, at another point she confronts her daughter aggressively, becomes violent and locks her up, beats and slaps her, sniffs her body for traces of his scent, accuses Duras of being a whore, less than a dog.

> Dans des crises ma mère se jette sur moi, elle m'enferme dans la chambre, elle me bat à coups de poing, elle me gifle, elle me déshabille, elle s'approche de moi, elle sent mon corps, mon linge, elle dit qu'elle trouve le parfum de l'homme chinois, elle va plus avant, elle regarde s'il y a des taches suspectes sur le linge et elle hurle, la ville à l'entendre, que sa fille est une prostituée, qu'elle va la jeter dehors, qu'elle désire la voir crever et que personne ne voudra plus d'elle, qu'elle est déshonorée, une chienne vaut davantage. (73)

> In her fits, my mother throws herself at me, shuts me up in the bedroom, beats me with her fists, she slaps me, she strips me, she comes near me, she smells my body, my underwear, she says that she finds the Chinese man's scent, she goes further, she looks to see if there are any suspicious stains on my underwear and she screams, the city can hear her, that her daughter is a prostitute, that she is going to throw her out, that she wants to see her die and that no one will ever want her again, that she is dishonored, that a bitch is worth more.

If the picture in *L'Amant* of Duras's fitfully mad mother confirms the one drawn in *Un barrage contre le Pacifique,* what of Stretter, who is entirely absent from that novel? La Dame, as the children nickname her, does not appear to exercise the same fascination over Duras in her earlier texts. What is different here is that Duras elaborates in greater detail an image of the young man who killed himself for love of Stretter. His image detaches itself with some force from these pages in which Duras describes the mendiante and her mother. This is a trio whose salient traits are madness, indifference, and death-inflicting sensuality and desire. Stretter and the beggar-woman are poles anchoring and augmenting those intolerable aspects of Duras's mother: her terrifying madness, absence, and interdiction against pleasure.

La Dame came from Savannakhet with her husband who was posted to Vinhlong. She remained incognita during the first year and a half of her husband's mission. "A cause de ce jeune homme, administrateur-adjoint à Savannakhet. Ils ne pouvaient plus s'aimer. Alors il s'était tué d'un coup de revolver" (109). (Because of the young man, an official in Savannakhet, they could no longer be lovers. So, he had killed himself with a shot from a revolver.) Duras remarks that she and Stretter share the isolation of women who possess this lethal, corporeal power.

La même différence sépare la dame et la jeune fille au chapeau plat des autres gens du poste. . . . Isolées toutes les deux. Seules, des reines. Leur disgrâce va de soi. Toutes deux au discrédit vouées du fait de la nature de ce corps qu'elles ont, caressées des amants, baisées par leurs bouches, livrées à l'infamie d'une jouissance à en mourir, disent-elles, à en mourir de cette mort mysérieuse des amants sans amour. (111)

The same difference separates the woman and the young girl with the flat hat from the other people of the post. Isolated, both of them. Alone, queens. Their disgrace goes without saying. Both to devalorization destined because of the nature of this body that they have, caressed by lovers, kissed by their mouths, delivered up to the infamy of an orgasmic pleasure whose intensity kills, to die from this mysterious death of lovers without love.

This projected identification confirms La Dame's importance, the alternative she provided to a less tolerable maternal model. The beggar-woman, who is mentioned only fleetingly in *Un barrage contre le Pacifique* but whose story is a full-blown framed fiction in *Le Vice-consul,* here receives her fullest description. She marks the other extreme in this trio. Tall and thin as death, the madwoman of Vinhlong runs barefoot, laughing and shouting. Unmistakably the beggar-woman of the novels and films. Duras recounts that her fear was so great in seeing this woman running behind her on one of the long avenues of Vinhlong that she was struck dumb and speechless. "Elle court en criant dans une langue que je ne connais pas. La peur est telle que je ne peux pas appeler. Je dois avoir huit ans. J'entends son rire hurlant et ses cris de joie, c'est sûr qu'elle doit s'amuser de moi. Le souvenir est celui d'une peur centrale. Dire que cette peur dépasse mon entendement, ma force, c'est peu dire" (103–4). (She runs while yelling in a language that I do not know. My fear is such that I cannot call out. I must be eight years old. I hear her screaming laughter and her yells of joy, it is clear that she is having fun with me. The memory is that of a gut fear. To say that this fear exceeds my understanding, my strength, this is saying very little.) The fear is one of contagious madness. After announcing the stupefying effect of this experience, Duras recounts, immediately and with no transition, another fear, that of seeing her mother's state so aggravated that she would be separated from her children. "Tard dans ma vie je suis encore dans la peur de voir s'aggraver un état de ma mère—je n'appelle pas encore cet état—ce qui la mettrait dans le cas d'être séparée de ses enfants" (104). (Late in my life I am still fearful of seeing a state of my mother become aggravated—I do not yet have a name for this state—which would put her in the situation of being separated from her children.) It is this terrifying threat of separation from her mother which fuels the terror inspired by the beggar-woman.

Duras describes her mother's slow sinking into her own madness as a sudden effacement of the person in whose stead there remains only an image. This passage of *L'Amant* poignantly expresses Duras's despair at her impotence to prevent the loss of a mother which she describes as a visual fading worthy of a primitive's fear of photographs.

> J'ai regardé ma mère. Je l'ai mal reconnue. Et puis, dans une sorte d'effacement soudain, de chute, brutalement je ne l'ai plus reconnue du tout. Il y a eu tout à coup, là près de moi, une personne assise à la place de ma mère, elle n'était pas ma mère, elle avait son aspect, mais jamais elle n'avait été ma mère. . . . L'épouvante ne tenait pas à ce que je dis d'elle de ses traits, de son air de bonheur, de sa beauté, elle venait de ce qu'elle était assise là même où était assise ma mère lorsque la substitution s'était produite, que je savais que personne d'autre n'était là à sa place qu'elle-même, mais que justement cette identitié qui n'était remplaçable par aucune autre avait disparu et que j'étais sans aucun moyen de faire qu'elle revienne, qu'elle commence à revenir. Rien ne se proposait plus pour habiter l'image. Je suis devenue folle en pleine raison. Le temps de crier. J'ai crié. (105–106)

> I looked at my mother. I did not recognize her very well. And then, in a sort of sudden erasure, fall, brutally I no longer recognized her at all. There was suddenly, there, near me, a person sitting in the place of my mother, she was not my mother, she looked like her, but she had never been my mother. . . . The horror did not come from what I say about her, her features, her air of happiness, her beauty, it came from the fact that she was sitting there where my mother had been sitting when the substitution happened, that I knew that no one else but she was there, in that place, but that precisely this identity which was replaceable by no other had disappeared and that I was without any means to make it return, make it begin to return. Nothing any longer offered to come and inhabit this image. I went mad in complete sanity. The time to scream. I screamed.

In her momentary shock of recognition that her mother was mad, Duras resembles her as she never seems to have before. She reacts to the unbearable effacement with a scream. Screams punctuate Duras's oeuvre, beneath language, despair and protest operating in concert. Thus, Duras flees this madwomen and finds solace in an imagined commonality with La Dame. Theirs is a sensual, lethal pleasure. While Stretter danced (reminiscent of the ball scene) he shot himself in the main square "étincelante de lumière" (112). A cinematic simulacrum, this image of a body crumpling in the middle of a glowing square recalls the multiple windows, doorways, and film screens with which Duras sets off the most intense fantasies of her characters. The body will be visited by the day, by the sun, and will finally be hauled away, leaving no trace. Like the body of the German soldier in *Hiroshima mon amour.* A young man's dead body, a trigger for the sentiment of loss. A body that circulates in the Durasian imagination and texts.

> C'était à la fin de la nuit qu'il s'était tué, sur la grande place du poste étincelante de lumière. Elle dansait. Puis le jour était arrivé. Il avait contourné le corps. Puis le temps passant, le soleil avait écrasé la forme. Personne n'avait osé approcher. La police le fera. A midi, après l'arrivée des chaloupes de voyage, il n'y aura plus rien la place sera nette. (112)

> It was at the end of the night that he had killed himself, on the shimmering central square of the post. She was dancing. Then the day had risen. It had circumscribed the body. Then, time passing, the sun had disfigured the form. No one had dared to approach. The police will do so. At noon, after the arrival of the travel boats there will be nothing anymore, the square will be clean.

The verbs in the passage chart time past to a progressive present to a future tense. The suicide, the body's destruction and its eventual removal are narrated with a sudden, typically Durasian intrusion of what seems to be direct discourse. The narrator's spatial and temporal coordinates are disorientingly unclear. What is clear, and striking, is the stark relief of this image. The suicide has already taken place; what is important to Duras is the corpse and its removal. For it is always the moment of separation from a corpse that traumatizes her heroines and her when she recounts the memories in which a young man's death triggers an overwhelming impression of loss. This is true in the Stretter memory recalled earlier, and when Duras comments on her brother's death. In the case of her brother, Duras equates his body with her own. "Personne ne voyait clair que moi. Et du moment que j'accédais à cette connaissance-là, si simple, à savoir que le corps de mon petit frère était le mien aussi, je devais mourir. Et je suis morte" (128). (No one saw things clearly but me. And from the minute that I realized this fact, so simple, which is to say that the body of my little brother was mine as well, I had to die. And I died.) Thus, the description of Stretter's victim may be considered, with its telltale marks of visual framing and dramatic lighting characteristic of fantasies and film screens, a fiction empowered with the intensity of another death. An overdetermined latchkey image in the Durasian imagination, circulating, a part of another drama.

Did she love him? Pivot asked this question of Duras about her lover. When a young male passenger on the ship carrying Duras to France hurls himself into the sea, she understands that she loved him. "Au cours d'un voyage, pendant la traversée de cet océan, tard dans le nuit, quelqu'un était mort. . . . [I]l y avait un jeune homme et, à un moment donné, ce jeune homme, sans un mot, avait posé ses cartes, était sorti du bar, avait traversé le pont en courant et s'était jeté dans la mer" (136). (During the trip, during the crossing of this ocean, late at night, someone had died. There was a young man and at a given moment, this young man, without a word, had put down his cards, had left the bar, had crossed the bridge, running, and had thrown himself into the sea.) But Duras quickly corrects herself as the body circulates in the imagination. This young man, a passenger on the ship in the version she has given Pivot and describes in *L'Amant*, is not a passenger but the son of the administrator in Sadec. Or is he Stretter's victim? Or is he her brother? In all cases, the devastation is expressed by a particular landscape comprising the rising sun, the empty space (of the sea, of the square, of the window) and the separation. "Le bateau était reparti à l'aube. Le plus terrible c'était ça. Le lever du soleil, la mer vide, et la décision d'abandonner les recherches. La séparation" (137). (The boat had departed again at dawn. The worst was that. The rising of the sun, the empty ocean, and the decision to abandon the search. The separation.) It is this separation from a body that triggers Duras's epiphany about her separation from her lover/ brother's body. An epiphany she recounts, as if watching herself as a character in the drama, in the third person.

> Et la jeune fille s'était dressée comme pour aller à son tour se tuer, se jeter à son tour dans la mer et après elle avait pleuré parce qu'elle avait pensé à cet homme de Cholen et elle n'avait pas été sûre tout à coup de ne pas l'avoir aimé d'un amour qu'elle n'avait pas vu parce qu'il s'était perdu dans l'histoire comme l'eau dans le sable et qu'elle le retrouvait seulement maintenant à cet instant de la musique jetée à travers la mer. (138)

> And the young girl had stood up as if to go, in her turn, kill herself, throw herself in her turn into the sea and afterwards she had cried because she

had thought of this man from Cholen and she had suddenly not been sure not to have loved him with a love that she had not seen because it had been lost in the story like water in the sand and she only found it now in this moment of music hurled across the sea.

The lover was not entirely lost to Duras. At least, his voice affirmed to her, over the telephone, that his passion would die with him. The final image of the work is that of this phone call. A conversation recounted in the third person, Duras's debased literary tense for memories purged of passion or passions betrayed by narration. The effect of terminating with this image is curious. For there the text opens with a photo and closes with a disembodied voice. It reaffirms the familiar image/sound disjunction while presenting a necessarily incomplete, unrepresentable picture of profound passion.

The mobility of and parallels between Duras's narration of different memories, the intensity of her passions, the writing style with its characteristic undulating rhythms and expanding repetitions, the fragmented and hallucinatory environment in which the language breathes with a respiratory tempo, all this enthralls. Duras is a writer for our times even as she continues to polarize her readers and befuddle pigeonholers. Her prodigious nostalgia and fascination with pieces of her own memories and her fixation of fantasmatic fictions place her squarely in the literature of narcissism and might diminish her readability were it not for her insistence on the political and historical dimension of her work, her contestation of human suffering. Here, Duras moves beyond the personal, merges the dolorous and ecstatic (usually feminine) generally expressed as madness into a paean to what she deems to be fundamental human passions, sexuality, and death. True to her own modernity, her filmic and literary language pose the limits of representation. Her language abuts memory, temporal and spatial signposts become illegible, all is pared to an essential and visionary simplicity. Duras's oeuvre taken in its largest and most radical aspect dismantles traditional text-making operations, while remaining profoundly anchored in real experience.

Notes

Chapter 1. Presenting Marguerite Duras

1. Duras claims that her political affiliations prevented the committee from giving her the prize in 1948, when *Un Barrage contre le Pacifique* was among the finalists. She was a Communist at the time. "Apostrophes," 28 September 1984, Antenne 2 (French television station).

2. Marcelle Marini pertinently points out that many of the critics, whose published remarks figured in the press packet of articles that *Editions de Minuit* assembled and put out to accompany *L'Amant*, stressed the confessional aspect and not the literary aspect of this work. Her argument is part of a longer polemic in which she is engaged regarding Duras's critical reception in general. See Marini, "Une Femme sans aveu," p. 6 and footnote 4.

3. For a bibliography/filmography of works through 1980, see Lyon, "Marguerite Duras." *Camera Obscura* 6 (Fall 1980), 50–55. For a filmography/bibliography current through 1983, see Entretiens de Marguerite Duras avec Dominique Noguez, in the publication accompanying the videocassette collection, *Oeuvres cinématographiques edition vidéographique critique* (Paris: Maison des Relations Extérieures, 1983).

4. "The postwar reputation of the American novel prompted many a writer, including Marguerite Duras, to attempt a type of fiction that betrays . . . the influence of Hemingway" (Cismaru, *Marguerite Duras,* [New York: Twayne, 1971] p. 17). "Marguerite Duras began, then, by drawing in some measure her inspiration from the American novel. . . . It is well perhaps to insist somewhat on that *Barrage* (1950) [*sic*] which placed Madame Duras in the front ranks of the young French novelists" (Armand Hoog, "Itinerary of Marguerite Duras," *Yale French Studies* 25. For further elucidation about the relationship between Hemingway and Duras, see Steinmetz-Schunemann, *Die bedeutung der zeit in den romanen von Marguerite Duras.*

5. The early debates were never well-resolved, according to Ouellet.

L'expression "Nouveau Roman" n'est ni heureuse ni originale pour désigner un ensemble d'oeuvres qui présentent indéniablement certaines analogies entre elles, mais n'en sont pas moins le plus souvent fort éloignées les unes des autres. . . . Presque tous les critiques des années 1955 ont rivalisé d'imagination pour coiffer d'un titre original cette nouvelle forme romanesque: Ecole du Regard, Chapelle de Minuit, Romans de la Table Rase, Romans blancs, Anti-ou Ante-Romans. . . . Mais seule l'expression 'Nouveau Roman' est demeurée et l'on ne voit pas qu'elle disparaisse bientôt (*Critiques de notre temps,* [Paris: Garnier, 1972] p. 7).

('New Novel' is neither a felicitous nor an original formulation by which to designate a group of works which, undeniably, display certain analogies between them but are no less, more often than not, very different from one another. Almost all of the critics in 1955 competed to find an original designation for this new novelistic form: The School of the Eye,

The Chapel of [the publishing house of Editions de] Midnight, Novels of the Tabula Rasa, White Novels, Anti- or Ante-Novels. But only the expression New Novel has remained and probably won't disappear any time soon.)

6. *Esprit* 7–8, p. 18.

7. Sarraute is linked with the "psychologizing" tendancy of the new novel school because of her "sous-conversations." Alain Robbe-Grillet's "phenomenological," or highly visual and descriptive style, came to define a wing of the school in which the subjective point of view was difficult to ascribe to any narrating consciousness. If Sarraute preserves an individual psychology in the new novel, Robbe-Grillet does not do less so. These distinctions are of questionable use, particularly given the tremendous voyeurism of Robbe-Grillet's narrators whose subjectivities certainly dominate their narratives.

8. Saporta remarks, "Au demeurant, ce qui permet de rattacher Duras au Nouveau Roman, à partir des années 50, c'est semble-t-il, une démarche extrême-ment mobile, ressortissant à la méthode du "point du vue," l'accent mis sur la disjonction entre le regard et la chose regardée (la procédé est particulièrement sensible dans certains films, comme *India Song*, où le regardant apparaît sans l'objet regardé), le recours au personnage en creux, la dé-réalisation et la technique du doute" ("Le Regard et L'Ecole," p. 49).

(What allows us to include Duras in the New Novel, from the fifties onward, seems to be an extremely mobile manner, an offshoot of the 'point of view' method, with the emphasis placed on the disjunction between the observer and the object seem (this procedure is particularly palpable in certain films, such as *India Song*, where the viewing subject appears without the seen object), the use of the withdrawn character, derealisation, and the technique of doubt.)

9. See Cismaru, *Marguerite Duras*, and Hoog, "Itinerary," particularly the in-troduction and conclusion, pp. 70, 72.

10. Murdick, "Sarraute, Duras, Burroughs, Barthelme and a Postscript." "It is difficult to take Mme Duras seriously. . . . None of it makes any sense, muses the superlatively uninteresting lunatic heroine of *The Ravishing of Lol V. Stein*" (pp. 478–9).

11. Duras and Gauthier, *Parleuses*, p. 60.

12. *Ibid.*, p. 13. Subsequently, in a television interview on "Apostophes" with Bernard Pivot, Duras reiterated that she had worked in silence for ten years. "Ça a duré dix ans, le silence autour de moi."

13. The post-Goncourt prize winner by Marguerite Duraille, *Virginie Q.* (Paris: Editions de Balland, 1988).

14. Noguez, "Gloire des mots," p. 26.

15. *Ibid.*, p. 29.

16. *India Song* is the most elaborate example of the plural reincarnations of a text. First commissioned by Peter Brook for the London theatre as a play in 1972, it was later produced on French radio. Next, it was produced as a film and finally, its sound track was used for a different visual film the following year.

17. Duras and Gauthier, *Parleuses*, p. 15.

18. Van Wert, "The Cinema of Marguerite Duras. "Duras has refined her cine-matic form, gradually eliminating concrete references for symbolic ones, restricting the camera's movement and the editor's arbitrary eclipse—cuts for long, repetitive takes and for fixed frames that are both boring and fascinating. . . . Why are her films so difficult, so boring, yet so important and so rewarding?" (p. 22).

19. Mothers are everywhere in Duras's work. A number of female protagonists are

mothers whose affective ties with their children are passionate and unarticulated. See, for example, *Détruire dit-elle*, the figure of the beggar-woman in *Le Vice-consul*, Anne-Marie Stretter and Lol Stein (both as daughter and mother) in *Le Ravissement de Lol V. Stein, Un Barrage contre le Pacifique*.

20. By psychoanalysis and psychoanalytic, I mean to include with Freud's work that of his disciples, colleagues, and successors, many of whom dissented from him. In specific instances of Freudian or Lacanian vocabulary, the sources will be cited. These are to be taken as examples of a dispensation first systematized by Freud.

21. In the five transcribed interviews with Xavière Gauthier (who uses Freudian language much more freely than does Duras) Duras employs terms such as *trauma* and *primal scene*. Describing her early memories of Anne-Marie Stretter, a central figure in the Indian Cycle, Duras says: "En tout cas, c'est comme la scène primitive dont parle Freud. C'est peut-être ma scène primitive, le jour où j'ai appris la mort du jeune homme" (85). Elsewhere she speaks about "Le trauma initial de toute femme" (159)—"Elle est dans le monde du désir, Anne-Marie Stretter" (215) Describing her female protagonists, she says, "Toutes mes femmes. [*sic*] Elles sont envahies par le dehors, traversées, trouées, de partout par le désir" (232). Duras and Gauthier, *Parleuses*.

(In any case, it is like Freud's 'primal scene.' Perhaps it is my primal scene, the day when I learned of the young man's death.

The first trauma of every woman.'

She is in the world of desire, Anne-Marie Stretter.

All of my women. They are invaded by the outside, traversed, pierced everywhere by desire.)

22. Duras's work elicits the interest of French psychoanalyst-literary critics such as Lacan, and Michèle Montrelay, for example.

23. See Brooks, "Fictions of the Wolfman," p. 75.

24. There is an expanding literature on the literariness of Freud's case histories and the way in which he is influenced by literary models. See, for example, Marcus, "Freud and Dora;" and Katz, "Speaking Out Against the "Talking Cure.'"

25. See Freud, "Analysis Terminable and Interminable." Standard Edition, vol. 23.

26. This is the general thrust of Marini's criticism of critics who refuse to acknowledge that Duras's work is anchored in her own experience, her desires and passions—political and sexual. See "Une Femme sans aveu" and "Marguerite Duras."

27. McCormick, "*India Song*."

28. See, for example, the recent cover article in the *New York Times Magazine*, "Literary Feminism Comes of Age," featuring Elaine Showalter. The article charts the rise of feminist criticism and its acceptance within the hallowed walls of academe. That the *New York Times* covered this story indicates how well institutionalized feminist criticism has become!

29. "J'écrivais comme on va au bureau, chaque jour, tranquillement; je mettais quelques mois à faire un livre et puis, tout à coup, ça a viré. Avec *Moderato* c'était moins calme. . . . Ça a été une rupture en profondeur. J'ai continué à mener une vie mondaine et puis un jour. . . . petit à petit, plutôt, ça a cessé complèment" (Duras and Gauthier, *Parleuses*, pp. 14, 59).

(I used to write like you go to the office, every day, peacefully. I took a few months to write a book and then, suddenly, things changed. With *Moderato*, it was less calm. There was a deep rupture. I continued to lead a social life and then, one day, little by little rather, it completely stopped.)

30. "Face à toute la société, elle a toujours refusé ce qu'on lui avait fait. . . ." (*Ibid.*, p. 83).

(Before all of society, she always refused what had been done to her.)

31. Ropars-Wuilleumier, "La mort des miroirs."

32. The three films—*La Femme du Gange* (1971), *India Song* (1975), and *Son nom de Venise dans Calcutta désert* (1976)—and the three novels—*Le Ravissement de Lol V. Stein* (1964), *Le Vice-consul* (1966), and *l'Amour* (1971), were first baptized by Ropars as the Indian Cycle.

33. D'autres [réalisations cinématographiques] prennent place au sein d'un ensemble plus vaste de textes liés les uns aux autres par un système de transformation permanente depuis *Le Ravissement de Lol V. Stein*, roman publié en 1964, jusqu'à *Son nom de Venise dans Calcutta désert*, film réalisé en 1976, l'écriture de Marguerite Duras n'a cessé de tourner autour d'une même histoire, à la fois originale et absente—résumable peut-être dans cette scène du bal qui, au début du *Ravissement*, fait s'échanger des couples liés les uns aux autres par le regard (Ropars, "Mort des miroirs," p. 4)

(Other [films] are situated at the heart of a larger group of texts tied together by a system of permanent transformation, beginning with *The Ravishing of Lol V. Stein*, novel published in 1964, up to *Her Venitian Name in Deserted Calcutta*, film made in 1976. Marguerite Duras's writing has not stopped revolving around the same story, at once originary and absent—summed up, perhaps, in the ball scene at the beginning of *The Ravishing* in which couples, linked to each other by their look, are exchanged.)

34. For a fuller development of a psychoanalytic interpretation of the relationship between spectator and film image, see Christian Metz, *Le Signifiant imaginaire: psychanalyse et cinéma* (Paris: U. G. E., 1977).

35. Jacques Lacan, "Hommage, . . . le seul avantage qu'un psychanalyste ait le droit de prendre de sa position, lui fût-elle donc reconnue comme telle, c'est de se rappeler avec Freud qu'en sa matière, l'artiste toujours le précède et qu'il n'a donc pas à faire le psychologue là où l'artiste lui fraie la voie" *Cahiers Renaud—Barrault* 52 (12/65). (p. 9).

(The only advantage that a psychoanalyst can take from his position, were it recognized as such, is to recall along with Freud that an artist always precedes him and that he has no right to play the psychologist there where an artist frays the path.)

36. Duras, *Moderato cantabile*. Page references are to the 10 / 18 edition.

37. Duras and Gauthier, *Parleuses*, p. 13.

38. *Ibid.*, p. 59.

39. Brée describes the son as "le centre de gravité dans la vie affective d'Anne Desbaresdes" in "Quatre romans de Marguerite Duras," p. 34. (the center of gravity in the affective life of Anne Desbaresdes).

40. Duras, *Moderato cantabile*.

41. Duras candidly comments on her alcoholism. "Je suis une alcoolique qui ne boit pas." (I am an alcoholic who does not drink.) She attributes the beginning of her alcoholism to a period when she went out regularly with men who encouraged her to drink. "Apostrophes," with Bernard Pivot. 28 September 1984, Antenne 2.

42. In her interviews with Pivot and Porte, Duras remarks that she was completely free as a child and ran wild through the forests and near the ocean while her mother was too distraught to supervise her.

43. For another example of bourgeois purgative vomiting, see Duras's *Détruire dit-elle*.

44. *Hiroshima mon amour*. The text is published as a screenplay and it is therefore justifiable speak of it as a text independent of the visuals.

45. Hell, "Univers romanesque de Marguerite Duras." Commentary following the text of *Duras*.

46. *Cahiers du Cinéma* 18:97 (July 1959): 1–18.

47. *Hiroshima* was Resnais's first feature-length film. Before it, he had made a number of art films and shorts with political themes: *Van Gogh* with Pierre Braunberger; *Gaugin; Guernica* (screenplay by Paul Eluard); *Les statues meurent aussi,* an anticolonialist film on the decline of African art, with Chris Marker (also of the New Wave generation); *Nuit et brouillard,* a return to the ruins of Nazi concentration camps, voice-over narration by Jean Cayrol; *Toute la mémoire du monde,* regarding the Bibliothèque Nationale in Paris; *Mystère de l'atelier quinze,* regarding the problems of industrial illness; and *Chant du Syrène,* regarding industrial toxics, narrated by Raymond Queneau.

48. According to Duras, the film was not an economic success for her because of her naïveté regarding film royalties. See her remarks to Gauthier in *Parleuses.*

49. Roy Armes, in *The Ambiguous Image: Narrative Style in Modern European Cinema,* observes that ". . . all of Alain Resnais' work can be seen—and indeed most usually has been seen—as a single meditation on time and memory" (p. 125).

50. Jacques Rivette observes that "la grande obsession de Resnais . . . c'est le sentiment de la fragmentation de l'unité première: le monde s'est brisé, il s'est fragmenté en une série de minuscules morceaux, et il s'agit de reconstituer le puzzle. [L]e cinéma, pour Alain Resnais, consiste à tenter de faire un tout avec des fragments *à priori* dissemblables . . . deux phenomènes concrets . . . liés uniquement parce qu'ils sont filmés en travelling à la même vitesse" (*Cahiers du Cinéma* 18: 97).

(Resnais' major obsession is the feeling of a fragmentation of the first unity. The world was splintered, fractured into a series of minute pieces and it is a matter of reconstructing the puzzle. The cinema, for Alain Resnais, is the attempt to make a whole with the pieces, ā priori dissimilar . . . two concrete phenomena brought together only because they are shot at the same speed in a traveling.)

51. Godard remarks, "On comprend tout ce qu'il a d'eisensteinien dans *Hiroshima,* car en fait, c'est l'idée profonde du montage, et même sa définition." *Cahiers du Cinéma* 18:97, p. 4.

52. Pierre Kast, *Cahiers du Cinéma* 18:97, p. 9.

53. Bowden, in an article on Alain Resnais in the *Oxford Companion to Film,* "*Hiroshima mon amour* contained striking innovations in the balance between words, music and image and even more in the treatment of narrative, past and present fluidly intermingling and subjective time being undifferentiated from the story's 'now.' His films are decidedly literary. Several of his scriptwriters have gone to make their own films, bringing French literature and cinema into a mutually enriching dialogue" (p. 591).

54. Sadoul, in *Dictionnaire des cinéastes,* states that "ce film, le plus important de la Nouvelle Vague française, connut un succès international mérité. . . . Le dialogue, trop littéraire de Marguerite Duras . . . devient un élément parmi d'autres" (p. 110). (This film, the most important of the French New Wave, warranted its international success. The overly literary dialogue of Marguerite Duras . . . becomes one element among others.) Before the New Wave, the French cinema of the 1950s consisted primarily of literary adaptations. Because this cinema was still governed by the classic conception of film as a visual medium, its literary origins had to be downplayed.

55. Chauvin similarly keeps Anne's glass filled while she pursues her fantasy about the couple.

Chapter 2. Fascinating Vision and Narrative Cure: *The Ravishing of Lol V. Stein*

1. Duras, *Ravissement de Lol V. Stein*. All translations are my own.

2. "Malgré le livre publié sous ce titre en 1973, . . . *la Femme du Gange*, . . . film tourné en 1972 et présenté confidentiellement en 1974" (trans. Ropars-Wuilleumier, "Contretextes," p. 83).

(Despite the book published in 1973 and entitled . . . *La Femme du Gange*. . . . a film made in 1972 and presented confidentially in 1974)

3. Duras and Gauthier, *Parleuses*, pp. 54–55.

4. "Le livre n'est pas assouvissant, ne clôt rien. Pour détruire ce qui est écrit et donc ne finit pas, il me faut faire du livre un film: le film est comme un point d'arrêt." Cover of *La Femme du Gange* from an interview with Benoît Jacquot, *Art Press*, October 1973.

(The book is not satisfying, it does not bring anything to closure. In order to destroy what is written and therefore does not end, I have to make a film from the book. The film is a stopping point.)

5. "On aurait cependant tort de voir là des adaptations ou des transcriptions—ou même un cycle. C'est un même texte, poursuivi, repris, obsessionellement repris, c'est l'épuisement des mêmes fantasmes [avec] son centre irradiant—le bal de S. Thala. . . ." Noguez, "India Songs de Marguerite Duras," p. 31.

(It would be incorrect to consider these as adaptations or transcriptions—or even a cycle. It is the same text, continued, reworked, obsessively reworked, it is the extenuation of the same fantasies [with] their irradiating center—the ball at S. Thala.)

6. "Et puis il y a ce couple que j'ai toujours négligé: Michael Richardson et Anne-Marie Stretter" (Duras and Gauthier, *Parleuses*, p. 55).

(And then there is this couple that I've always neglected: Michael Richardson and Anne-Marie Stretter)

7. "C'est curieux, mais cette espèce de personne qui est sortie d'ici, il y a huit ans, ou neuf ans, je ne sais plus, je ne peux pas faire croire que je la vois, donc je ne ferai pas de film, je le ferai avec des loques, des restes de Lol V. Stein, je peux travailler sur Lol V. Stein, avec ça seulement." Duras and Porte, *Lieux*, p. 101.

(It is odd, but this sort of person who came out of here eight or nine years ago, I can't persuade anyone that I see her, so I won't make a film, I'll make it with the tatters, the debris of Lol V. Stein, I can only work on Lol V. Stein with that.)

8. Ropars Wuilleumier, *L'Avant scène du cinéma* p. 5.

9. When discussing *L'Amour* with Xavière Gauthier, Duras identifies the madwoman as Lol Stein. "Elle [une lectrice] croyait que la femme habillée de noir de *La Femme du Gange*, c'était une autre Lol. V. Stein. A mon avis, non; à mon avis, c'est Tatiana Karl." (119) "Tous les quatre—le fou, le jeune homme, Lol. V. Stein et puis la femme en noir aussi." (121) "MD: Ah, la femme de *L'Amour*, c'est Lol. V. Stein." (199)

(A reader thought that the woman dressed in black of *La Femme du Gange* was another Lol V. Stein. In my opinion, no, in my opinion it's Tatíana Karl [119]. All four of them—the madman, the young man, Lol. V. Stein and then the woman in black also. [14]. MD: Oh, the woman in *L'Amour* is Lol. V. Stein.

10. Ropars-Wuilleumier, in *Texte divisé*, states à propos the differences between *India Song* and *La Femme du Gange*, "[L]e choix d'acteurs professionels connus et l'investissement dans les jeux chatoyants du miroir le distinguent évidemment de la pauvreté et de l'abstraction précédemment explorées avec *La Femme du Gange*, qui ne fut pas diffusé commercialement" (p. 127).

(The choice of professional and well known actors and the investment in the mirror's play of reflection, distinguish it, clearly, from the impoverishment and abstraction of *La Femme du Gange*, which was not commercially distributed.)

11. All accounts given here of *La Femme du Gange* are based on other spectators' comments. I have never seen the film. See, in addition to Ropars-Wuilleumier, Van Wert, "Cinema of Marguerite Duras."

12. Speaking about a shot in which a turbaned male, dressed in white, lights a lamp on a piano on which there is a photograph of a young woman and vase of flowers, Duras says, "Au milieu de l'image, en plein milieu de l'image, il y a ce que j'ai appelé l'autel, à la mémoire d'Anne-Marie Stretter. C'est un double lieu. C'est le mien, c'est à dire celui de ma douleur, la douleur de ne pas pouvoir la sortir de la mort, mort provoquée par moi, et c'est le lieu de mon amour d'elle" (Duras and Porte, *Lieux*, p. 72).

(At the center of the image, the very center, there is what I called the altar, in memory of Anne-Marie Stretter. It is a double site. It is mine, the altar of my suffering, the suffering of being unable to leave death, a death provoked by me, and it is the site of my love for her.)

13. This is the thesis that Jeanne-Marie Clerc explores in her "Le rapport des images et des mots." *Revue des Sciences Humaines* 202, pp. 103–116.

14. Théophano-Artémis Harziforou, in his *Présence de la voix. A propos de L'Homme Atlantique de M. Duras,* complains that "A propos de M. Duras on n'a que trop souvent parlé de ravissement et de fascination: d'une écriture fascinée et fascinante." (The terms ravishing and fascination or fascinated and fascinating writing have been used all too often a propos of M. Duras.) *Hors cadre* 6, (p. 94). But this is a question of chronology. The accumulated fatigue of seeing the same descriptions for the effect of Duras's writing is a particular problem for writers writing in the wake of earlier Duras criticism, rather than a measure of the inappropriateness of the term.

15. S. Tahla in the edition of the novel cited *ibid.*, and S. Thala in other references.

16. Duras and Porte, *Lieux de Marguerite Duras*, pp. 99–101.

17. *Ibid.*, p. 20.

18. Freud, in "Constructions in Analysis," asks: "What sort of material does [the patient] put at our disposal which we can make use of to put him on the way to recovering the lost memories? All kinds of things . . . fragments of these memories in his dreams . . . ideas . . . repetitions of the affects belonging to the repressed. It is out of such raw material . . . that we have to put together what we are in search of . . . [The analyst's] task is to make out what has been forgotten from the traces which it has left behind, or more correctly, to construct it" (p. 258).

19. It would be impossible for someone to suffer an originary trauma at the age of nineteen. Freud conceived of originary traumata as early sexual events, discovered and defined as traumata only retroactively. He began to write about traumata in his preliminary Communication of 1893; "On the Psychical Mechanism of Hysterical Phenomena." Two years later, in *Studies in Hysteria,* he argued that symptoms without apparent physiological cause, hysterial symptoms, were provoked by an early sexual assault incomprehensible as sexual abuse for the prepubescent child. Physiological maturity and sexual initiation gave the earlier event meaning retroactively. The unconscious memory generated a body language of symptoms. This is the sense of Freud's remarks that hysterics suffer mainly from reminiscences. Interpreting these symptoms led to a recall of the early event or events.

When told of sexual advances, Freud initially believed that his patients had been what today we would call abused. The abusers were usually their fathers or other close male relatives. In the late 1890s, however, Freud recanted the position that hysteria was provoked by real abuse. Correspondence with his admired friend, Dr. Wilhelm Fliess, documents his changes of heart. On 21 September 1897 (Letter 69) Freud describes his discomfort at generalizing from his patients' experiences to consider how many perverse fathers were at large. ". . . There was the astonishing fact that in every case . . . blame was laid on perverse acts by the father, and realization of the unexpected frequency of hysteria, in every case of which the same thing applied, though it was hardly credible that perverted acts against children were so general." In his footnote to this letter, Freud writes, This section was written while I was under the ascendency of an error which I have since then repeatedly acknowledged and corrected. I had not yet found out how to distinguish between patients' phantasies about their own childhood and real memories. I consequently ascribed to the aetological factor of seduction an importance and general validity which it does not possess. Nevertheless, there is no need to reject the whole of what appears in the text above; seduction still retains a certain aetiological importance." ("Further Remarks on the Neuro-Psychoses of Defence, 1896," and "The Specific Aeotiology of Hysteria," pp. 189–221).

The question is: How much? Did Freud refuse to accept the frequency of wide-spread child abuse to protect his own father, as some have claimed, or to protect Fliess? Would the hypothesis of infantile sexuality be put forth when the seduction theory "broke down under the weight of its own improbability and contradiction. . . ." ("Infantile Sexuality," p. 17). Relocating the sexual urge in the child helped Freud to explain how children could generate phantasies of sexual abuse that they later "remembered." Freud's consideration of the relative roles of the imagination and the material world, of exterior forces and internal sexual urges is one of his more long-standing concerns.

Jeffrey Masson is the latest to launch an assault on Freud's scientific judgment. See Masson and Janet Malcolm's account of the internecine wars following Masson's defection from the psychoanalytic ranks in *Inside the Freud Archives* (New York: Alfred Knopf and Co., 1984).

20. Montrelay, *Ombre et le nom*, p. 13.

21. Ropars-Wuilleumier points to what she considers to be the misplaced tenacity of the analytic interpretation of this scene as triangular. "Le vide insistant de la salle, le caractère faussement origine1 de la scène, précédée de l'évocation d'un préau "vide" où Tatiana et Lol dansaient le jeudi, l'inexistence même du spectacle que reconstitue Lol dans le champ de seigle n'ont pas suffi à faire reculer une inteprétation analytique selon laquelle le manque—fût-il dérobé—n'est que le signe inverse d'une plénitude assurant par ailleurs l'homogénéité de la représentation" ("Contretextes," p. 85).

(The insistent emptiness of the room, the falsely originary aspect of the scene, preceded by the "empty" courtyard where Tatiana and Lol danced on Thursdays, the very inexistence of a spectacle that Lol recreates in the rye field—none of these have forced back a (psycho)analytic interpretation according to which the lack—be it hidden—is nothing more than the other side of a plenitude which assures the homogeneity of the representation.)

22. According to Clément, "[L]e fantasme (a) . . . la fonction d'une cadre, la structure d'une logique. Object d'évocations rêveuses et point de fuite de la lit-térature le fantasme est devenu l'axe d'une possible formalisation analytique. [L]e fantasme . . . est scène. . . . Le scénario implique une fixité, un récit, un déroule-ment réglé: en même temps, le mot même induit la notion de scène constitutive à la structure fantasmatique. Le scénario se présente comme une succession de scènes" (*Pouvoir des mots*. pp. 89–90).

(Fantasy has the function of a frame, the structure of a logic. The object of dreamy evocation and vanishing point of literature, the fantasy has enabled an analytic formalization. Fantasy is a scene. The scenario implies something constant, a story, an ordered unfolding: at the same time, the word suggests the idea of a scene constituting the fantasmatic structure. The scenario offers itself as a series of scenes.)

23. According to Laplanche and Pontalis in their article, "Fantasme," a fantasy is "l'ensemble de la vie du sujet qui se révèle comme modelé, agencé par ce qu'on pourrait appeler, pour en souligner le caractère structurant, une fantasmatique. Celle-ci n'est pas à concevoir seulement comme une thématique . . . elle comporte son dynamisme propre, les structures fantasmatiques cherchant à s'exprimer, à trouver une issue vers la conscience, et attirant constamment à elles un nouveau matériel" (p. 155).

(The whole of a subject's life reveals itself to be shaped, structured by what we might call, in order to underscore the structuring character, a fantasmatic. This should not be conceived of as solely thematic for the fantasmatic has its own dynamic, and seeks conscious expression by constantly drawing upon new material.)

24. See Moustapha Safouan, *La Sexualité féminine dans la doctrine Freudienne.* Paris, Editions du Seuil, 1976.

25. "La fonction du stade du miroir s'avère pour nous dès lors comme un cas particulier de la fonction de *l'imago* qui est d'établir une relation de l'organisme à sa réalité. . . . Ce développement est vécu comme une dialectique temporelle qui décisivement projette en histoire la formation de l'individu: le *Stade du Miroir* est un drame dont la poussée interne se précipite de l'insuffisance à l'anticipation—et qui pour le sujet, pris au leurre de l'identification spatiale, machine les fantasmes qui se succèdent d'une image morcellée du corps à une forme que nous appelerons orthopédique de sa totalité,—et à l'armure enfin assumée d'une identité rigide tout son développement mental." "Le Stade du Miroir comme formateur de la fonction du Je" (Lacan, *Ecrits*, pp. 93–94).

(I am led, therefore to regard the function of the mirror-stage as a particular case of the function of the *imago,* which is to establish a relation between the organism and its reality. This development is experienced as a temporal dialectic that decisively projects the formation of the individual into history. The mirror stage is a drama whose internal thrust is precipitated from insufficiency to anticipation—and which produces for the subject, trapped by the image of spatial identification, a succession of fantasies extending from a fragmented body-image to a total form that I will call orthopedic—that will mark the armor of a rigid identity that is ultimately adopted.)

26. Lacan, "Hommage à Marguerite Duras," p. 10.

27. *Ibid.*

28. Barthes, *Fragments d'un discours amoureux,* p. 223.

29. Lacan, in *Four Fundamental Concepts of Psychoanalysis* asks: "Is it not remarkable that at the origin of the analytic experience, the real should have presented itself in the form of that which is unassimilable in it—in the form of the trauma. . . ." (p. 55).

30. ". . . il apparaît que le regard, porté sur le spectacle, est l'object même du fantasme . . . le fantasme réside dans l'optique elle-même. C'est le fantasme du *voir.* Qui redouble la nature du fantasme, s'il est vrai que celui-ci est d'abord une structure par où passe le regard, un cadre, un passage pour la vision, un défilé étroit où le sujet doit aménager ses objets" (Clément, *Pouvoir des mots,* pp. 98–100).

31. ". . . La fascination du récit fantasmatique . . . *récit-cadre* celui qui, comme le cinématographe, change sans cesse de *point de vue,* . . . rend impossible la localisation de l'énonciation: qui voit, qui regarde?" (Clément, *Pouvoir des mots,* p. 100).

32. Narrative must ever present itself as a repetition of events that have already

happened, and within this postulate of a generalized repetition it must make use of specific, perceptible repetitions in order to create plot, that is, to show us a significant interconnection of events. Events gain meaning by repeating (with variation) other events. Repetition is a return in the text, a doubling back. We cannot say whether this return is a return to or a return of. . . . Repetition through this ambiguity appears to suspend temporal process, or rather, to subject it to an indeterminate shuttling or oscillation. (Brooks, "Freud's Masterplot," *Yale French Studies* 55/6 (1977) p. 285).

Chapter 3. *Le Vice-consul* and *India Song:* Dolores Mundi

1. "Il a fallu que je passe par Lol pour arriver à *India Song.*" (I had to go through Lol to get to *India Song.*) "Couleur des Mots," Conversation avec Dominique Noguez following taped version of *India Song* published as a set of six films and accompanying commentary.

2. "Je l'ai fait se tuer pour m'en débarrasser." (I had her kill herself to rid myself of her.) Ibid.

3. Ropars-Wuilleumier, "Contretextes," p. 82.

4. On the sound track of *India Song*, the beggar-woman sings *Savannakhet* and not *Battambang*.

5. Théophano-Artémis Hatziforou, in "Présence de la voix: A propos de *L'Homme Atlantique* de M. Duras," observes that "A propos de M. Duras on n'a que trop souvent parlé de ravissement et de fascination: d'une écriture fascinée et fascinante. Quelque abusive qu'une telle attitude puisse paraître, elle trouve son explication dans une imprégnation sonore qui dépasse l'entendement immédiat, projetant les textes vers le supra ou l'infra-verbal . . . un texte oral." *Hors cadre* 6, pp. 94, 102.

(There has been too much discussion of ravishing and fascination, of a fascinated and fascinating style of writing style with respect to M. Duras. This excess can be explained by the total sonorousness of her work, which eludes immediate comprehension, projecting these texts toward a supra- or infra- verbal state—an oral text.)

6. See Marini's discussion of this scene in *Territoires du féminin*.

7. Published as a "texte théâtre film" in 1973, commissioned by Peter Hall for the British National Theatre, then later recorded for French radio and finally released as a film in 1975. See Duras and Gauthier, *Paleuses*, p. 185.

8. Duras and Porte, *Lieux*, p. 91.

9. Ibid.

10. Duras, *India Song*, p. 10.

11. "Ainsi découpée, l'éconciation verbale ne peut trouver de support diégétique à l'image. . . . Plus l'image se tait . . . plus l'attention se porte sur l'énoncé des voix, seule base sémantique quand la représentation fait défaut. La tentation serait grande de conclure à une possible disjonction, et de suivre en cela les propositions mêmes de Duras. . . . Mais c'est là précisément que le sépartisme rencontre ses limites: qu'une même piste sonore puisse engendrer deux films radicalement différents ne désigne pas seulement la polysémie d'une bande-son capable de supporter deux types de lecture; la possibilité d'une telle représentation indique plus fortement que l'écriture du film détruit l'identité de la bande-son: plus le film s'écrit, plus la structuration filmique procède de l'articulation ménagée par la structure interne à ces énoncés, pour une bande-son montée, jamais de bande à part. *Le Texte Divisé*, pp. 140–41.

(Thus separated, the verbal enunciation is not supported by the image. As the image becomes increasingly silent, attention is increasingly accorded to what the voices say, the only semantic base when the representation falters. It would be tempting to argue for a possible disjunction, and to agree with Duras. But it is here that separatism encounters its limits: that a single sound track can generate two radically different films affirms the polysemism of a sound track capable of producing two types of readings; moreover, the possibility of such a representation reinforces the identity of the sound track. As the film is increasingly written, the filmic structuration increasingly moves toward an articulation overseen by the internal structure of what is said. For an articulated sound track, never an independent sound track.)

See also, Chion who argues that in "un film comme *India Song* . . . Marguerite Duras supprime presque complètement le son in tout en usant largement du son horse-champ: on n'entend parler les personnages qu'une fois qu'on les a vus sortir. Mais c'est ce 'presque' qui en fait toute la force. Apparemment, en effet, le film ne fait entendre que du son hors-champ (les voix des protagonistes sortis du cadre, l'orchestre invisible du bal de la réception à laquelle nous assistons)—ou bien du son off (d'autres voix qui parlent au pas) des personnages que nous voyons ou une musique de piano de Beethoven). Il y a cependant, au coeur du film, une illusion de son in quand on voit le couple d'Anne-Marie Stretter et du Vice-Consul qui danse lentement . . . et qui se parle. On pourrait presque croire voir remuer les lèvres mais il n'en est rien: les bouches et Delphine Seyrig et Michael Lonsdale, les acteurs, restent closes. On ne sait si l'on entend une conversation imaginaire ou télépathique, ou s'ils se sont dit ces choses-là ailleurs ou dans un autre temps. . . ." (Chion, *Son au Cinéma*, pp. 40–41.

(In a film such as *India Song* . . . Marguerite Duras suppresses in sound almost entirely while using a good deal of off screen sound: we hear characters speak once we have seen them leave the screen. But it is this "almost" which creates the effect. The film, apparently, only lets us hear off screen sound [the voices of the characters outside the frame, the invisible orchestra at the ball of the reception which we see]—or off sound [other voices speaking in time] of characters we see or of piano music by Beethoven. There is, however, at the heart of the film, one illusion of sound in when we see Stretter and the vice-consul dancing slowly . . . and speaking to each other. We can practically believe that we see their lips moving, but it is not the case. The mouths of Delphine Seyrig and Michael Lonsdale, the actors, remain closed. We do not know if we are listening to an imaginary or telepathic conversation, or if they have spoken to each other elsewhere or in another time.)

12. "In a film, a sound is considered 'off' (literally off the screen) when in fact it is the sound's source that is off the screen, therefore an 'off screen voice' is defined as one which belongs to a character who does not appear (visually) on the screen. We tend to forget that a sound in itself is never 'off': either it is audible or it doesn't exist." Christian Metz, "Aural Objects," *Yale French Studies* 60 (1980): p. 29.

Michel Chion asserts that "*[J]amais le son en lui-même . . . servirait à situer le son, lequel est naturellement chose diffuse, mêlée, aux frontières indécises.* Nous conserverons donc, dans cette étude, des critères de localisation et de regroupement des sons choisis *en fonction de l'image et de ce qu'elle indique*, parce qu'il n'y en a pas d'autres possibles ou plutôt parce que le cinéma, c'est un jeu qui—même chez Godard, Duras ou Michaël Snow—se joue comme ça, par rapport à l'espace d'un écran investi comme lieu de pas-tout-voir." Chion, *Son au cinéma*, p. 30.

(*Sound in itself never situates the sound which is naturally diffuse, mixed, with unclear boundaries.* We will keep the criteria of localization and regrouping of sounds *as a function of the image and what it indicates,* because there are no other criteria or, rather, because cinema is a game that—even in Godard's, Duras's or Michael Snow's work—is played like that, with respect to the space of the screen invested as a place where not everything is seen.)

13. Noel Burch, writing about the dialectic of on and off space in *Praxis du Cinéma,* explains the impossibility of their being simultaneously on screen—that is, the impossibility of the cinema's presenting a whole world. He refers to Bonitzer, "*Voici,*" *Cahiers du cinéma,* 273 (February 1977).

14. "[T]ous ceux qui ont posé ou qui ont discuté cette distinction n'ont pas manqué de dire qu'elle était incomplète, et que la musique du film, par exemple, ou la voix-off du commentateur-narratuer n'ont pas le même statut que la musique du pianiste invisible qui est le voisin des personnages . . . ou que la voix du personnage que le changement d'axe de la caméra a rejeté en dehors du champ, mais non de l'action, et qui continue son discours." Chion, *Son au cinéma,* p. 32.

(Everyone who has raised or discussed this distinction has said that it was incomplete, and that film music or the voice-over of a narrator/commentator, for example, do not have the same status as the music of an invisible pianist who is next to the characters . . . or the voice of a character moved off screen by a different camera angle but still in in terms of the action, and who continues what he is saying.)

In *Praxis du Cinéma,* Burch introduces a temporal dimension by offering the terms imaginary and concrete to define a sound corresponding to an image which was once off, but easily imaginable as contiguous to on space, and then on.

15. "*Son hors-champ,* seulement celui *dont la cause n'est visible simultanément* dans l'image, *mais qui reste pour nous situé* imaginairement *dans le même temps que l'action montrée et dans un espace contigu à celui que montre le champ de l'image; . . . son off,* seulement celui qui *émane d'une source invisible située dans un autre temps et/ou un autre lieu* que l'action montrée dans l'image (musique du film, voix-off du narrateur racontant l'action au passé.) Ce qui, avec le son "in" dont nous conservons la définition courante, nous donne *trois cas:* un cas de son "visualisé" et deux cas de son 'acousmatique'. . . ." Ibid.

(Off-screen [hors-champ] sound is only that sound whose cause is not simultaneously visible in the image, but which remains, for us, imaginarily situated in the same time as the action we are seeing and in a space contiguous to the space shown in the field of the image; off sound, only that which emanates from an invisible source situated in another time and/or place than the action shown in the film [film music, voice over of the narrator telling the story in the past tense]. With in sound, whose generally accepted definition we retain, we have three cases: a case of visualized sound and two cases of acousmatic sound.)

16. Ibid., chap. 3, "Le point d'écoute."

17. Panofsky remarks that "film art is the only art the development of which men now living have witnessed from the very beginning." "Style and Medium in the Motion Pictures," p. 15.

18. The literature exploring and theorizing the relationship between film and language, between films and novels, between filmic organization and linguistic structures, is extensive. Michel Marie puts it succinctly. "Aujourd'hui encore, alors que la parole est au centre de l'écriture filmique tant chez Marguerite Duras que chez Jean-Luc Godard, Jean-Marie Straub, elle garde toujours sa tache originelle, sa connotation impure au sein de l'idéologie critique envisagée globalement: le film, cela reste l'image." "Le Film, la parole et la langue," p. 69.

(Even today, where language is the center of filmic writing as much in the work of Marguerite Duras as that of Jean-Luc Godard and Jean-Marie Straub, it retains its original stain, its impure connotation, as the heart of a globally conceived critical ideology: film remains the image.)

19. Eisenstein's statement, signed by Pudovkin and Kuleshov as well, strongly urged contrapuntal sound in order to preserve the integrity and hegemony of the image. "[E]very adhesion of sound to a visual montage piece increases its inertia as a montage piece, and increases the independence of its meaning. Only contrapuntal use of sound in relation to the visual montage piece will afford a new potentiality of montage development and perfection. The first experimental work with sound must be directed along the line of its distinct non-sychronization with the visual images." *Film Form*, p. 258.

20. Jean-Louis Baudry describes this process of transformation, or work, as cinematographically specific, that is, as differentiating cinema from other systems of signification. See Baudry, "Ideological Effects of the Basic Cinematographic Apparatus."

21. "S'il existe une idéologie de la représentation, à laquelle souscrirait en quelque sorte mécaniquement le cinéma, on pourrait en pointer le symptôme le plus radical et en même temps le plus inaperçu dans la disposition première qui fait de tout individu un spectateur, et qui consiste, au cinéma, d'abord à investir la surface de l'écran d'une fictive profondeur." Bonitzer, *Regard et la voix*, p. 9.

(If there is an ideology of representation to which cinema would mechanically subscribe, its most radical and least noticed symptom lies in the primary disposition which makes of every individual a spectator. At the cinema, this consists of initially investing the surface of the screen with a fictive depth.)

22. "In the cinema the camera carries the spectator into the film picture itself. We are seeing everything from the inside as it were and are surrounded by the characters of the film. . . . Nothing like this "identification" has ever occurred as the effect of any other system of art and it is here that the film manifests its absolute artistic novelty." Balázs, *Theory of the Film*, p. 48.

23. "Le miroir est le lieu de l'identification primaire. L'identification au regard propre est secondaire . . . mais elle est fondatrice du cinéma et donc primaire lorsqu'on parle de lui: c'est proprement l'identification cinématographique primaire. . . . Quant aux identifications aux personnages avec elles-mêmes leurs différents niveaux (personnage hors-champ, etc.,) ce sont les identifications cinématographiques secondaires, tertaires, etc.; si on les prend en bloc pour les opposer simplement à l'identification du spectateur à son regard, leur ensemble constitue, au singulier, l'identification cinématographique secondaire." Metz, *Signifiant imaginaire*, p. 79.

(The mirror is the site for primary identification. Identifying with a look is secondary . . . but it is a founding gesture when it comes to the cinema, and therefore primary. . . . Regarding identification with characters each with their different levels [off screen character, etc.,] these are secondary, tertiary identifications, etc. If we take them as a whole to oppose them simply to the identification of a spectator with his own gaze, they constitute a secondary cinematographic identification.)

24. "Ce 'recul' critique ressemble beaucoup à une défense contre 'l'impression de réalité', contre la puissance d'assertion dont on crédite le cinéma. C'est une défense, dans la mesure où le geste en reste liée, et même aliène, à 'réalisme' du détail, du décor, etc. appuyant la 'vraisemblance' du récit, qui obsède le cinéma classique. . . . Le réel constitue la borne idéologique autour de laquelle tourne la critique, la lecture dévisée et bloquée, entre l'hésitation névrotique et le tourniquet fétichiste (le déni) où alternent les paradigmes du 'vrai' et du 'faux'. Cette alternance du 'judgement' de la lecture et de sa dérive, c'est à dire de sa productivité, définit sommairement le

mécanisme de la captation spec(tac)ulaire; la 'prise de distance' est un moment nécessaire de la représentation, qui permet de prévoir, de tolérer et de maîtriser les chutes de 'crédibilité." Bonitzer, "Le hors-champ (Espace en défaut.)" p. 15.

(This critical distance greatly resembles a defense against the "impression of reality," against the strength of assertion with which the cinema is credited. It is a defense insofar as the gesture is tied to and even alienates the "realism" of the detail, the decor, etc., emphasizing the "verisimilitude" of the tale which haunts classical cinema. The real is the ideological boundary around which the criticism turns, a reading divided between a neurotic hesitation and a fetishistic [denial] where paradigms of "true" and "false" alternate. This alternation of the "judgement" of the reading and its straying, that is to say, its productivity, summarily defines the mechanism of spec[tac]ular captation. Setting oneself at a distance is a necessary moment in the representation that allows the spectator to foresee, tolerate, and master the breakdowns of credibility.)

Similarly, Metz claims that [p]our comprendre le film de fiction, il faut à la fois que je "me prenne" pour le personnage (= démarche imaginaire), afin qu'il bénéficie par projection analogique de tous les schèmes d'intelligibilité que je porte en moi, et que je ne me prenne par pour lui (= retour au réel) afin que la fiction puisse s'établir comme telle (= comme symbolique): c'est le *semble-réel.*" *Signifiant imaginaire*, p. 80.

(In order to understand the fiction film, I must take myself for the character [= imaginary procedure] so that he benefits, by analogical projection, from all the patterns of intelligibility which I possess, and at the same time that I do not take myself for the character [= return to reality] so that the fiction can be established as such [− as symbolic]: it is the *seems-real.*)

Laura Mulvey also suggests an oscillation between two spectatorial positions of identification and denial. "[T]he cinema has structures of fascination strong enough to allow temporary loss of ego while simultaneously reinforcing the ego." "Visual Pleasure and Narrative Cinema," p. 10.

25. See the excellent discussion regarding theatrical illusion in Mannoni, "L'Illusion cominque ou le théâtre du point de vue de l'imaginaire," *Clefs pour l'Imaginaire*, pp. 161–84.

26. "La fonction du stade du miroir s'avère pour nous dès lors comme un cas particulier de la fonction de *l'imago* qui est d'établir une relation de l'organisme à sa réalité. Ce développement est vécu comme une dialectique temporelle qui décisivement projette en histoire la formation de l'individu: *le Stade du Miroir* est un drame dont la poussée interne se précipite de l'insuffisance à l'anticipation—et qui pour le sujet, pris au leurre de l'identification spatiale, machine les fantasmes qui se succèdent d'une image morcellée du corps à une forme que nous appelerons orthopédique de sa totalité,—et à l'armure enfin assumé d'une identité rigide tout son développement mental." Lacan *Ecrits I,* "Le Stade du Miroir comme formateur de la fonction du Je," pp. 93–94.

(I am led, therefore, to regard the function of the mirror-stage as a particular case of the function of the *imago*, which is to establish a relation between the organism and its reality. This development is experienced as a temporal dialectic that decisively projects the formation of the individual into history. The mirror stage is a drama whose internal thrust is precipitated from insufficiency to anticipation—and which produces for the subject, trapped by the image of spatial identification, a succession of fantasies extending from a fragmented body-image to a total form that I will call orthopedic—that will mark the armor of a rigid identity that is ultimately adopted.)

27. In his *Three Essays on Sexuality* of 1905, Freud links scopophilia to touch and

makes the eye an erotogenic zone. Later, he argues that this produces pleasure in watching spectacles. In the "Fourth Lecture on Psychoanalysis," he argues that "instinctual components of sexual pleasure . . . occur in pairs of opposites, active and passive . . . most important representative of this group [are the] active and passive desire for looking, from the former of which curiosity branches off later on and from the latter the impulsion to artistic and theatrical display." *Standard Edition* 11, p. 44.

28. Mulvey argues that "the fascination of film is reinforced by pre-existing patterns of fascination already at work within the individual subject and the social formations that have moulded him." "Visual Pleasure and Narrative Cinema," p. 6.

29. "En poussant les choses jusqu'au bout, on en viendrait à admettre que, chez l'adulte, les effets de masque et ceux de théâtre sont possibles en partie grâce à la présence de processus qui s'apparentent à ceux de la négation (*Verneinung*); qu'il faut que ce ne soit pas vrai, que nous sachions que ce n'est pas vrai, afin que les images de l'inconscient soient vraiments libres. Le théâtre, à ce moment, jouerait un rôle proprement symbolique." Mannoni, *ibid.*, p. 166.

(Taking things to their limit, we would agree that for the adult, the effects of a mask and of the theatre are possible thanks, in part, to the presence of processes related to those of negation [*Verneinung*]. It is necessary that it not be true, that we know that it is not true, in order to free unconscious images. Thus, theatre would play a properly symbolic role.)

30. Bonitzer defines the mood of this film as nostalgic. "La musique, le parfum, le rêve dont ces noms sont chargés, et la date, 1937. Voyons, mais ce charme, quel est-il? Mais oui, bien sûr, cela crève les yeux: la mode rétro! La mode rétro. Rétro veut dire nostalgique." *Le Regard et la voix*, p. 149.

31. Marie-Claire Ropars Wuilleumier's precise segmentation differentiates pro-logue (30 minutes; shots 1–27) from story (57 minutes; shots 28–58) from epilogue (23 minutes; shots 59–72) based on the changes of voices on the sound track. Grange proposes three divisions, based on the changing position of the narrators with respect to the image: contiguous in Part I, unified with the image in Part II, and distant from the image and transparent in Part III. See Grange, "Un système d'écriture," pp. 51–59. Marie offers an analysis of the film based on the degrees of distance between the voices and a potential speaking subject, suggesting "une typologie marquant cinq degrés de distance vis à vis d'un éventuel sujet de l'énonciation externe ou interne à la fiction . . . voix de narrateurs . . . intemporelles . . . voix des invités anonymes . . . des personnages désignés par la bande sonore . . . personnages présents à l'image ne parlant jamais (Michael Richardson) . . . personages présents à l'image censés dia-loguer. . . . Marie, "La parole dans le cinéma contemporain," p. 46.

(A typology indicating five degrees of distance with respect to an eventual speaking subject exterior or interior to the fiction: intemporal narrative voices; voices of anonymous guests; characters designated by the sound track; characters whom we see but who never speak [Michael Richardson]; characters whom we see and whose ostensible voices we hear.)

32. Chion describes the impression of a strong bond between sounds and images as nostalgic. "L'image ici n'accueille jamais aucun son, mais en même temps tous les sons semblent se presser sur ses bords, nostalgiques d'un lieu qui les délivrerait de leur errance. Le champ filmé, dans *India Song*, agit pour les sons comme *foyer de fascination* autour duquel ils sont réunis sans pouvoir s'y perdre. . . ." Chion, *Son au cinéma*, p. 42.

(The image never receives any sound, but at the same time all the sounds seem to rush to its edges, nostalgic for a space which would deliver them of their wandering.

The filmed space, in *India Song*, acts like a foyer of fascination around which the sounds converge, unable to lose themselves in it.)

33. Laplanche and Pontalis, *Vocabulaire de la psychanalyse*, p. 152.

34. Clément, *Miroirs du Sujet*, p. 100.

35. Clément argues that "le fantasme (a) . . . la fonction d'un cadre, la structure d'une logique. Objet d'évocations rêveuses et point de fuite de la littérature, le fantasme est devenu l'axe d'une possible formalisation analytique. [L]e fantasme . . . est scène. . . . Le scénario implique une fixité, un récit, un déroulement réglé: en même temps, le mot même induit la notion de scène constitutive à la structure fantasmatique. Le scénario se présente comme une succession de scènes." Clément, *Pouvoir des Mots*, pp. 89–90.

(Fantasy has the function of a frame, the structure of a logic. The object of dreamy evocations and the vanishing point of literature, fantasy has become the axis of a possible psychoanalytic formalization. A fantasy is a scene. The scenario implies a story, a logical unfolding, a permanence. At the same time, the word suggests the notion of a scene which establishes a fantasmatic structure. The scenario offers itself as a succession of scenes.)

36. "The gaze in itself not only terminates the movement, it freezes it. . . . What is . . . that time of arrest of the movement? It is simply the fascinatory effect, in that it is a question of dispossessing the evil eye of the gaze, in order to ward it off. The evil eye is the *fascinum*, it is that which has the effect of arresting movement and, literally, of killing life. At the moment the subject stops, suspending his gesture, he is mortified. The anti-life, anti-movement function of this terminal point is the *fascinum*, and it is precisely one of the dimensions in which the power of the gaze is exercised directly. The moment of seeing can intervene here only as a suture, a conjunction of the imaginary and the symbolic." Lacan, *Four Fundamental Concepts*, pp. 117–18.

37. In the chapter on *La Ravissement de Lol V. Stein*, I situated Lol at the periphery of the Imaginary and Symbolic. Recalling this, it is interesting to note Clément's remarks about Lacan's definition of fantasy. "Ainsi le fantasme est à la conjonction de l'imaginaire, reflet instable et du symbolique, cadre obligé du langage. C'est ce que Lacan désigne par la formule $\emptyset$ a . . . ◇. Ce poinçon est le cadre du fantasme, ce qui dans les scènes hystériques se représente par la porte entrouverte, la lucarne dans la nuit, la fenêtre géante; cadre du désir. . . . Il fonde un rapport impossible entre le sujet et l'objet du désir: identité et non-reciprocité absolue, dans laquelle le sujet est déterminé par un objet auquel il ne peut avoir aucun accès." Clément, *Miroirs du Sujet*, p. 99.

(The fantasy is thus at the intersection of the imaginary, unstable reflection, and of the symbolic, necessary frame of language. This is what Lacan means by the formula $\emptyset$ a . . . ◇. The diamond is the frame of the fantasy, which is represented in hysterical scenes by an open doorway, a light in the night, an enormous window: the frame of desire. It establishes an impossible relationship between the subject and object of desire: identity and absolute non-reciprocity in which the subject is determined by an object to which there is no access.)

38. Laplanche and Pontalis suggest that fantasies figure a subject's answers to the questions of his or her origins. "Fantasmes des origines dans le scène primitive, c'est l'origine de l'individu qui se voit figurée; dans les fantasmes de séduction c'est l'origine, le surgissement de la sexualité; dans les fantasmes de castration, c'est l'origine de la différence des sexes." Laplanche and Pontalis, "Fantasmes originaires," p. 1854.

(Fantasies of origins in the primal scene are figures of the individual's origins; in seduction fantasies, it is the origin, the surge of sexuality; in castration fantasies, it is the origin of sexual difference.)

39. "[L]e fantasme n'est texte qu'en partie; il a à se formuler comme texte, sous la forme d'un énoncé insistent dans le discours su sujet . . . mais cet énoncé, sur lequel une sémiotique peut intervenir, n'est sans doute que le résultat de l'operation fantasmatique, indissolublement texte et scene." Clément, *Pouvoir des Mots*, p. 91.

(A fantasy is only a text in part. It must be formulated as a text, in the form of an insistent énoncé in the subject's discourse. But this énoncé, upon which a semiotic operation can intervene, is doubtless the result of a fantasmatic operation, indissociably text and scene.)

Chapter 4. Autographies and Fictions

1. Duras and Porte, *Lieux*, pp. 64–69.
2. Duras et al., *Marguerite Duras*, p. 85.
3. Moustapha Safouan, *Sexualité féminine dans la doctrine freudienne*, p. 30.
4. Although Duras has said that she is not sure of Stretter's name, she has identified her with Elisabeth Striedter, the wife of the administrator who arrived from Laos when Duras was eight years old. Striedter's daughters contacted Duras when their mother was ninety-three years old and in a retirement home in Fontenay-les-Roses. "C'était à Vinhlong, en Cochinchine, où ma mère était institutrice d'école indigène. Un jour, l'administrateur a été nommé dans un autre poste. Un nouvel administrateur est arrivé du Laos avec sa femme et ses deux filles. La première fois que cette femme entre dans un de mes livres, j'ai quarante ans, c'est en 1964, dans *Le Ravissement de Lol V. Stein*. Le personnage principal de ce livre-là n'est cependant pas Anne-Marie Stretter, mais Lola Valérie Stein. Mais je sais qu'Anne-Marie Stretter, c'est Elisabeth Striedter. Elle devient Anne-Marie Stretter en 1965, dans *le Vice-Consul*. Et reste de ce nom-là dans le film *India Song*, en 1975" (*Marguerite Duras Oeuvres Cinématographiques*, p. 21).

(It was in Vinhlong, in Indochina, where my mother was a school teacher for the local population. One day, an administrator was named to another post. A new administrator arrived with his wife and two daughters, from Laos. The first time that this woman enters into one of my books, I am forty, it is in 1964, in *Le Ravissement de Lol V. Stein*. The main character of that novel, however, is not Anne-Marie Stretter, but Lola Valerie Stein. But I know that Anne-Marie Stretter is Elisabeth Streidter. She becomes Anne-Marie Stretter in 1965, in *Le Vice-consul*. And keeps the same name in the film, *India Song*, in 1975.)

5. "Déjà *l'Amant* venait rappeler que l'oeuvre s'enracinait dans une vie concrète de femme; dans une histoire liée à un milieu familial et social singulier appartenant à un espace et à une époque spécifiques (une famille de pauvres blancs pendant la colonisation française en Indochine entre les deux Guerres.)" Marini, "Marguerite Duras: Une nouvelle écriture du politique," p. 36.

(*L'Amant* already reminded us that Duras's work is rooted in the concrete life of a woman, in a history tied to a particular familial and social milieu that belonged to a specific space and time [a family of poor whites during France's colonization of Indochina between the two Wars.])

6. Marini, "Pas un vide mais une vie pleine; pas un récit vide mais à partir d'un vide la possibilité chaque fois d'un récit plein à sa façon. Une sorte de provocation au

nom de l'écriture autobiographique créatrice d'un espace en dehors de l'opposition du réel et de l'imaginé." *Ibid.*, p. 36.

(Not a void, but a full life, not an empty story but, starting with a void, the possibility, each time, of a story, full in its own way. A sort of provocation in the name of autobiographic writing that creates a space outside of the opposition between the real and the imagined.)

7. "Je suis créole, je suis née là-bas." Pivot, "Apostrophes," 28 September 1984, Weekly television show on Antenne 2 of French national television.

(I am a creole, I was born there.)

8. See Porte, *Lieux,* pp. 56–61, and Pivot, "Apostrophes."

9. See Duras and Gauthier, *Parleuses,* p. 177.

10. Duras and Porte, in *Lieux,* observe that "elle a déraillé à ce moment-là, elle a fait des crises épileptiformes. Elle a perdu la raison. On a cru qu'elle allait mourir. Je crois que c'était de colère à vrai dire qu'elle voulait mourir. . . . De colère. D'indignation. Evidemment, ça nous a terriblement marqués. Je ne peux même pas encore en parler calmement, voyez." Duras tells Pivot that "elle était folle de naissance, dans le sang. Je ne peux pas vous dire en quoi elle l'était." Pivot, *Ibid.*

(she went off at that point she had epilepsy-like fits. She lost her reason. We thought she was going to die. I believe that she wanted to die of rage, in truth. Of rage. Of indignation. Obviously this deeply marked us. I still can't talk about it calmly, you see.) she was mad from birth, in her blood. I can't tell you just how she was.)

11. "Ce sont mes berceuses, l'histoire de la concession." *Ibid.* (Those are my lullabies, the story of the concession.)

12. Duras, *A Sea of Troubles.* English translations from this edition marked by page numbers.

13. Duras and Gauthier, *Parleuses,* p. 136.

14. "Mon frère était beau et il jouait bien au tennis. Alors il y avait une exception pour lui." Duras et al., *Marguerite Duras,* p. 84.

(My brother was handsome and he played tennis well, so there was an exception made for him.)

15. "J'ai vu cette femme avant tout comme une donneuse de mort. "*Marguerite Duras Oeuvres Cinématographiques,* p. 21.

(I saw this woman above all as a giver of death.)

16. "Oh! j'étais un microbe, j'avais sept ans. Attends, c'était peut-être plus tard, peut-être que j'avais jusqu'à onze ans là. Je ne peux pas te dire, me souvenir bien." Duras et. al., *Marguerite Duras,* p. 84.

(Oh! I was a shrimp, I was seven. Wait, maybe it was later, maybe I was as old as eleven. I cannot tell you, I cannot remember clearly.)

17. Duras and Porte, *Lieux,* p. 64.

18. *Ibid.,* p. 65.

19. *Marguerite Duras Oeuvres Cinématographiques.* p. 21

20. Pivot, "Apostophes."

21. *Ibid.*

22. *Ibid.*

23. Duras and Porte, *Lieux,* p. 65.

24. Duras explains in *L'Amant* that La Dame, as Stretter was called, broke off a liaison with young administrateur-adjoint in Savankhet before leaving with her husband who was being posted to Vinhlong. Her young lover killed himself.

25. Duras and Porte, *Lieux,* pp. 64–65.

26. Gauthier asks Duras a propos of her memory of the accident. "Mais tu penses que ça peut être un souvenir, ça ne pourrait pas être un fantasme?" "Non. J'en suis sûre." *Parleuses*, p. 85.

(But do you think that it can be a memory, couldn't it be a fantasy? No. I am certain.)

27. *Ibid.*

28. Duras reiterates this in her interviews with Dominique Noguez: "C'est une chose qui m'avait beaucoup bouleversée. Comme si ma scène primitive à moi passait par la mort. Anne-Marie Stretter était aussi bien donneuse de mort que mère d'enfant, mère de petites filles de mon âge, huit ans, huit ans et demi." *Marguerite Duras Oeuvres Cinématographiques*, p. 21.

(It is something that really overwhelmed me. As if my primal scene included death. Anne-Marie Stretter was a giver of death as well as a mother, the mother of young girls my age, eight and a half.)

29. "Evidemment, dans *Le Barrage*, je voulais pas raconter tout. Je voulais que ce soit harmonieux. On m'avait dit: "Il faut que ce soit harmonieux." Duras and Gauthier, *Parleuses*, p. 139.

(Obviously, in *The Sea Wall*, I did not want to tell everything. I wanted it to be harmonious. They had told me, 'Make it harmonious.')

30. Duras reports that her mother, like all French colonials, was a racist. Because of her racism, she would have been unable to tolerate her daughter's affair with a Chinese man. This would have been more traumatic for her than the story of the failure of her sea wall. And, Duras tells Pivot, this is no small claim. Pivot, "Apostophes."

31. Duras has said that she and her brother never lived on the concession but always in the apartments reserved for the schoolteacher, an arrangement still practiced today by the French government.

32. Duras, *Sea of Troubles*.

33. In *The Imaginary Signifier*, Metz identifies a number of levels of identification between spectator and film image. His point of departure is a parallel between the film spectator and a dreamer who watches his dream. The filmgoer has the impression of watching images of his or her own creation. Primary identification is made between spectator and the camera whose "look" produces the image: secondary and tertiary identifications link spectator and characters who either look themselves or whose look is supposed by the image. See notes in preceding chapter. Mannoni, "L'illusion Comique ou le théâtre du point de vue de l'imaginaire," and "Je sais bien mais quand même;" Bonitzer, "Le hors-champ (Espace en défaut);" Metz, *Le Signifiant imaginaire*.

34. I am endebted to Borgomano's *Ecriture filmique de Marguerite Duras* for its excellent discussion of the conjunction of cinema and desire in this novel.

35. Duras and Porte, *Lieux*. Duras says, "à côté de moi, c'est mon frère, Joseph du *Barrage contre le Pacifique*. Il est mort très jeune pendant la guerre, faute de médicaments." Caption of a photo of Duras and her brother, p. 46.

(Next to me is my brother Joseph, from *Barrage contre le Pacifique*. He died during the war, very young for want of medication.)

36. Interview with Annie Declerck [*sic*], "The Fruit of the Original Sin." Only Duras's voice is audible.

37. Pivot asks the question on "Apostrophes."

38. *Ibid.*

39. In her interview with Annie Declerck [*sic*], Duras says that "Il a éclipsé les

autres amours de . . . dans ma vie. Il était sans énoncé, sans déclaration, dans l'émotion, même physique."

(He eclipsed all the other loves of . . . in my life. He was without words, without declarations, in emotion, even in physical emotion.)

40. Dominique Noguez confirmed my intuition. Jean Mascolo, Duras's son and a photographer, asked his mother to write an introduction and commentary for their family photo album. Dura's comments on the absolute photo that was never taken were to introduce the album which was subsequently lost.

41. Claude Roy brings attention to this in his article, "Duras toute entière à la langue attachée," which appeared in *Le Nouvel observateur* 31 (August 1984), cited by Marini.

Bibliography

Alazet, Bernard. "Je m'appelle Aurélia Steiner." *Didascalies* 3, Cahiers occasionnels de l'ensemble théâtre mobile (April 1982): 50–61.

———. "L'embrasement, les cendres." *Revue des Sciences Humaines* 204. "Ecrivains dans la guerre" (1986-4): 147–60.

———. "Les roses de Versailles." In *Ecrire dit-elle, Imaginaires de Marguerite Duras,* edited by Danielle Bajomée and Ralph Heyndels, 153–64. Brussels: Editions de l'Université, 1985.

———. "Les traces noires de la douleur." *Revue des Sciences Humaines* 202: "Marguerite Duras" (1986-2): 37–51.

Altman, Rick. "Moving Lips: Cinema as Ventriloquism." *Yale French Studies* 60 (1980): 67–79.

Amar, David, and Pierre Yana. "Sublime, forcément-sublime. A propose d'un article paru dans *Libération.*" *Revue des Sciences Humaines* 202. "Marguerite Duras" (1986-2):153–65.

Armes, Roy. *The Ambiguous Image: Narrative Style in Modern European Cinema.* Bloomington and London: Indiana University Press, 1976.

Bal, Miecke. *Narratologie: Essais sur la signification narrative dans quatre romans modernes.* Paris: Klincksieck, 1977.

Balàzs, Béla. *Theory of the Film: Character and Growth of a New Art.* New York: Dover Publications, 1970.

Barthes, Roland. *Fragments d'un discours amoureux.* Paris: Seuil, 1977.

———. "Rhétorique de l'image." *Communications* 4 (1964): 40–51.

Baudry, Jean Louis. "Ideological Effects of the Basic Cinematographic Appartus." Translated by Alan Williams from *Cinéthique* 7/8 (1970): 1–8 as "Ideological Effects." *Film Quarterly* 27:2 (Winter 1974–75): 39–47.

———. "The Apparatus." Translated by Jean Andrews and Bertrand Augst. *Camera Obscura* 1 (1976): 104–26.

Belmans, J. "Un cinéma de la durée romanesque." *Synthèses* 76 (1969): 122–30.

Benassy, M., and R. Diatkine. "Ontogenèse du fantasme." *Revue française de psychanlayse* 4 (1964): 539–65.

Benveniste, Emile. *Problèmes de linguistique générale* 1. Paris: Gallimard, 1966.

Bernheim, Nicole-Lise. *Marguerite Duras tourne un film.* Paris: Editions Albatross, 1975.

Besnard-Coursodon, M. "La signification du métarécit dans *Le Vice-Consul* de Marguerite Duras." *French Forum* 3 (1978): 72–83.

Bishop, Lloyd. "The Banquet Scene in *Moderato cantabile*." *Romanic Review* 69:3 (1978): 222–35.

Bonitzer, Pascal. "La notion de plan et le sujet du cinéma. Voici." *Cahiers du cinéma* 273 (January–February 1977): 5–17.

———. "Le hors-champ (Espace en défaut)." *Cahiers du cinéma* 234–35 (December 1971–January–February 1972): 8–16.

———. *Le Regard et la voix*. Paris: Union Générale d'Editions, 1976.

Borgomano, Madeleine. *L'Ecriture filmique de Marguerite Duras*. Paris: Albatros, 1985.

Bowden, Liz-Anne, ed. *Oxford Companion to Film*. New York and London: Oxford University Press, 1976.

Braudy, Leo. *The World In a Frame: What We See in Films*. New York: Doubleday, 1977.

Brée, Germaine. "Quatre romans de Marguerite Duras." *Cahiers Renaud Barrault* 52 (December 1965): 23–39.

Brooks, Peter. "Fictions of the Wolfman: Freud and Narrative Understanding." *Diacritics* 9:1 (1979): 72–81.

———. "Freud's Masterplot." *Yale French Studies* 55/6 (1977).

Burke, Edmund. *A Philosophical Enquiry into the Origin of Our Ideas of the Sublime and Beautiful*. Edited by James T. Boulton. London: Routledge & Kegan Paul, 1958.

Butor, Michel. *Essais sur le roman*. Paris: NRF Gallimard, 1960.

Casey, Ed. "The Memorability of the Filmic Image." *Quarterly Review of Film Studies* 6:3 (Summer 1981): 241–64.

Chapsal, M. "Les Femmes Folloes." *La Quinzaine littéraire* 24 (1967).

Chateau, Dominique et al., ed. *Cinémas de la modernité: films, théories*. Paris: Klincksieck, 1981.

Chatman, Seymour. "Towards a Theory of Narrative." *New Literary History* 6:2 (Winter 1975): 295–318.

Chiland, Colette. "Le Statut du fantasme chez Freud." *Revue française de psychanalyse* 2–3 (1971): 203–15.

Chion, Michel. *Le Son au cinéma*. Paris: Seuil, 1985.

Cismaru, Alfred. *Marguerite Duras*. New York: Twayne, 1971.

———. "Marguerite Duras and the New Novel." *Dalhousie Review* 47 (1967–68): 203–13.

Cixous, Hélène. "The Laugh of the Medusa." In *New French Feminisms*, edited by Elaine Marks and Isabelle de Courtivron, 245–65. Amherst: University of Massachusetts Press, 1980.

Clément, Catherine. *Miroirs du sujet*. Paris: Union générale d'editions, 1975.

———. *Le Pouvoir des mots: symbolique et idéologique*. Paris: Réprères Mame, 1973.

Clerval, Alain. "Duras et Sa Liturgie." Review of *L'homme assis dans le couloir. le Nouvel observateur*, 2 August 1980, 50.

Cohen, Susan. "La Présence de rien." *Cahiers Renaud Barrault* 106 (1983): 17–36.

Cohn, Dorritt. *Transparent Minds: Narrative Modes for Presenting Consciousness in Fiction*. Princeton: Princeton University Press, 1978.

Copjec, Joan. "*Indian Song/Son nom de Venise dans Calcutta désert:* The Compulsion to Repeat." *October* 17 (Summer 1981): 37–53.

Dallenbach, Lucien. *Le Récit spéculaire: essais sur la mise en abyme.* Paris: Seuil, 1977.

Daney, Serge et al., ed. "Marguerite Duras: les yeux verts." *Cahiers du cinéma* (June 1980): 312–13.

Dawson, Jan. "*India Song:* A Chant of Love and Death." Interview with Marguerite Duras. *Film Comment* 11:2–12:1 (November–December 1975): 52–55.

Doane, Mary Anne. "The Voice in the Cinema: The Articulation of Body and Space." *Yale French Studies* 60 (1980): 33–50.

Duras, Marguerite. *L'Amant.* Paris: Editions de Minuit, 1984.

———. *L'Amour.* Paris: Gallimard, 1971.

———. *Un barrage contre le Pacifique.* 13th ed. Paris: Gallimard, 1958.

———. Hiroshima mon amour: scénario et dialogue. Paris: Gallimard, 1960.

———. *India Song: Texte, Theatre, Film.* Paris: Gallimard, 1973.

———. *Moderato cantabile.* Paris: UGE, 1958.

———. *Moderato cantabile.* Translated by Richard Seaver in *Four Novels by Marguerite Duras.* New York: Grove Press, 1965.

———. Duras and Noguez, commentary following films, collected as *Oeuvres cinématographiques. edition vidéographique critique.* Paris: Maison des Relations Extérieures, 1983.

———. *Le Ravissement de Lol V. Stein.* Paris: Gallimard (Collection soleil), 1964.

———. *A Sea of Troubles.* Translated by Antonia White. Harmondsworth: Penguin Books, 1969.

———. *Le Vice-consul.* Paris: Gallimard (Collection l'imaginaire), 1966.

———. *War: A Memoire.* Translated by Barbara Bray. New York: Pantheon Books, 1986. Published in France as *La Douleur.*

Duras, Marguerite et al. *Marguerite Duras.* Paris: Editions Albatros, 1975.

Duras, Marguerite and Xavière Gauthier. *Les Parleuses.* Paris: Editions de Minuit, 1974.

Duras, Marguerite and Michelle Porte. *Les Lieux de Marguerite Duras.* Paris: Editions de Minuit, 1977.

Eisenstein, Sergei. *Film Form and the Film Sense: Essays in Theory.* Edited and translated by Jay Leyda. Cleveland and New York: World Publishing, 1957.

Erens, Patricia, ed. *Sexual Strategems: World of Women in Film.* New York: Horizon Press, 1979.

Felman, Shoshana. "Women and Madness: The Crtical Phallacy." *Diacritics* (Winter 1975): 2–11.

Forrester, Viviane. "Ecriture et cinéma: Marguerite Duras." *Art Press* 43 Dossier Cinéma (December 1980): 7–8.

Frank, Joseph. *The Widening Gyre.* New Brunswick, N.J.: Rutgers University Press, 1963.

Freud, Sigmund. *The Origins of Psychoanalysis: Letters to Wilhelm Fliess: Drafts and Notes, 1887–1902.* Translated by Eric Mosbacher and James Strachey. New York: Basic Books, Inc., Publishers, 1954.

———. *Standard Edition.* 24 vols. Edited by James Strachey. London: Hogarth Press, 1953.

Friedman, A. W. *Multivalence: The Moral Quality of Form in the Modern Novel.* Baton Rouge and London: Louisiana State Press, 1978.

Genette, Gérard. *Figures* II. Paris: Tel Quel, 1969.

Girard, René. "Scandal and the Dance: Salomé in the Gospel of Mark." Paper delivered at the Symposium on Interpretation and Creativity. University of Chicago, 6 April 1982.

Glassman, Deborah. "The Feminine Subject as History Writer in *Hiroshima mon amour.*" *Enclitic* 5:1 (Spring 1981): 45–53.

Graham, Peter, ed. *The New Wave.* New York: Doubleday & Company, 1968.

Grange, Marie-Françoise. "Un système d'écriture: *India Song* de Marguerite Duras." *Ça cinéma* 19 (Paris: Albatross, 1980): 51–59.

Guicharnaud, Jacques. "Woman's Fate: Marguerite Duras." *Yale French Studies* 24 (1960): 106–20.

Harvey, Sir Paul, ed. *Oxford Companion to Classical Literature.* Oxford: Clarendon Press, 1962.

Hauser, Arnold. *Social History of Art* IV. New York: Vintage Books, 1960.

Heath, Stephen. *Nouveau Roman: A Study in the Practice of Writing.* Philadelphia: Temple University Press, 1972.

Hell, Henri. "L'univers romanesque de Marguerite Duras." Commentary following *Moderato Cantabile*, by Marguerite Duras. Paris: Edition de Minuit (Collection 10/18), 1958.

Houg, Armand. "The Itinerary of Marguerite Duras (or, From the Dangers of the American Novel to the Perils of the Abstract Novel, Without Mishap.)" *Yale French Studies* 29 (1960): 68–72.

Husserl-Kapit, Susan. "An Interview with Marguerite Duras." *Signs* 1:2 (Winter 1975): 423–34.

Isaacs, Susan. "The Nature and Function of Phantasy." *International Journal of Psychoanalysis* 29:2 (1948): 73–93.

Johnston, Claire, ed. *Notes on Women's Cinema.* London: Society for Education in Film and TV, 1973.

Kahler, Erich. *Inward Turn of Narrative.* Translated by Richard and Clara Winston. Princeton: Princeton University Press, 1973.

Kanters, Robert. "Un bal chez Marguerite Duras." *Le Figaro Littéraire*, 3 February 1966, p. 5.

Kast, Pierre, *et al.* "*Hiroshima* notre amour." *Cahiers du Cinéma* 18:97 (1959): 1–18.

Katz, Susan. "Speaking Out Against the 'Talking Cure:' Unmarried women in Freud's Early Case Studies." *Women's Studies* 13:4 (1987).

Kawin, Bruce. *Mindscreen.* Princeton, N.J.: Princeton University Press, 1978.

Kolbert, Elizabeth. "Literary Feminism Comes of Age." *New York Times Magazine* 6 December 1987, pp. 110–117.

Kracower, Sigfried. *Theory of Film.* New York: Oxford University Press, 1960.

Kristeva, Julia. "The Pain of Sorrow in the Modern World: The Works of Marguerite Duras." *PMLA* 192:2 (March 1987): 138–51.

Lacan, Jacques. *Ecrits* I. Paris: Seuil, 1967.

———. *Four Fundamental Concepts of Psychoanalysis.* Translated by Alan Sheridan. Edited by J. A. Miller. New York: Norton, 1977.

————. "Hommage fait à Marguerite Duras: *Le Ravissement de Lol V. Stein.*" *Cahiers Renaud-Barrault* 52 (December 1965): 7–15.

Laplanche, Jean and J. B. Pontalis. "Fantasme originaire, fantasme des origines, origine du fantasme." *Les Temps Modernes* 225 (April 1954): 1833–68.

————, eds. *The Language of Psychoanalysis.* Translated by Donald Nicholson-Smith. New York: W. W. Norton & Company, 1973.

Lotman, Juri. "Points of View in a Text." *New Literary History* 6:2 (Winter 1975).

Lyon, Elisabeth. "The Cinema de Lol V. Stein." *Camera Obscura* 6 (Fall 1980): 7–41.

————. "Marguerite Duras: Bibliography/Filmography. *Camera Obscura* 6 (Fall 1980): 50–55.

Mackward, Christiane. "Structures du silence/du délire: Marguerite Duras/Hélène Cixous." *Poétique* 35 (September 1978): 316–24.

Malcolm, Janet. *In the Freud Archives.* New York: Alfred Knopf, 1984.

Mannoni, Octave. *Clefs pour l'imaginaire ou l'autre scène.* Paris: Seuil, 1969.

Marcus, Steven. "Freud and Dora: Story, History, Case History." *Representations* (New York: Random House, 1975): 247–309.

Marie, Michel. "Le film, la parole, et la langue." *Cahiers du 20e siècle 19: cinéma et littérature.* Paris: Klincksieck, 1968.

————. "La parole dans le cinéma français contemporain: l'exemple d'*India Song; ça/cinéma*" 19 (Paris: Albatross, 1980).

Marini, Marcelle. "Marguerite Duras: Une nouvelle écriture du politique." *Il confronto litterario:* Quaderni del dipartimento de lingue e letterature straniere moderne dell'universita di Pavia. Supplementa al n. 8. (1988): 35–50.

————. "La mort d'une érotique." *Cahiers Renaud Barrault* 106 (1983): 37–57.

————. *Territoires du féminin avec Marguerite Duras.* Paris: Minuit, 1977.

————. "Une femme sans aveu." *L'Arc* 98 (Paris: Editions LE JAS, 1985): 6–15.

McCormick, Ruth. "*India Song:* The Play, the Film, Duras." *Focus* 1:7 (July–August 1981): 2.

Mellen, Joan. *Women and Their Sexuality in New Film.* New York: Horizon Press, 1973.

Mendilow, A. A. *Time and the Novel.* New York: Humanities Press, 1972.

Mercier, Vivian. *New Novel from Queneau to Pinget.* New York: Farrar, Strauss, & Giroux, 1966.

Metz, Christian. *Le Signifiant imaginaire: psychanalyse et cinéma.* Paris: Union Générale d'Editions, 1977.

————. "Aural Objects." *Yale French Studies* 60 (1980).

Micha, René. "Une seule mémoire." *NRF* 17 (1961): 297–306.

Michalczyk, John. *The French Literary Filmakers.* New Jersey: Art Alliance Press, 1980.

Monaco, James. *How to Read a Film.* New York: Oxford University Press, 1977.

Montrelay, Michèle. *L'Ombre et le nom: sur la féminité.* Paris: Editions de Minuit, 1977.

Mudrick, Marvin. "Sarraute, Duras, Burroughs, Barthelme and a Postscript." *Hudson Review* (Autumn 1967).

Mulvey, Laura. "Visual Pleasure and Narrative Cinema." *Screen* 16 (1975): 6–18.

Murphy, Carol J. "Duras' New Narrative Regions: The Role of Desire in the Films of Marguerite Duras." Paper delivered at the Sixth Annual Conference on film and literature. Florida State University, 28 January 1982.

Nadeau, Maurice. *Le Roman français depuis la guerre*. Paris: Gallimard, 1970.

Noguez, Dominique. "La Gloire des mots," *L'Arc* 98 Paris, Editions Le JAS, 1985, 24–40.

———. "Les India Song de Marguerite Duras." *Cahiers du 20e siècle 9: cinéma et litérature*. Paris: Klincksieck, 1978.

Orlando, F. *Towards a Freudian Theory of Literature*. Translated by Charmaine Lee. Baltimore: Johns Hopkins University Press, 1978.

Ouellet, Réalet, ed. *Les Critiques de notre temps et le nouveau roman*. Paris: Garnier, 1972.

Panofsky, Erwin. "Style and Medium in the Motion Pictures." In *Film: An Anthology*. Daniel Talbot, compiler. Berkeley: University of California Press, 1969.

Pivot, Bernard. "Apostrophe." Friday evening French television program on Antenne 2. Special program on Marguerite Duras, featuring interviews with her. 28 September 1984.

Prédal, René. "Marguerite Duras un livre—un film," edited by Jean Granarolo, 279–90. *Annales de la faculté des lettres et sciences humaines de Nice* 29. Monaco: Belles Lettres, 1977.

Ropars-Wuilleumier, Marie-Claire. "Contrextextes," ou le jeu de voix chez Marguerite Duras." *Revue des sciences humaines* 202:L Marguerite Duras (1986): 79–102.

———. "Disembodied Voice *(India song)*." *Yale French Studies* 60 (1980): 241–69.

———. "Duras." *Avant-scène du cinéma* 225 (1 April 1979).

———. *Le Texte divisé: Essai sur l'écriture filmique*. Paris: Presses Universitaires de France, 1981.

Rose, Jacqueline. *Sexuality in the Field of Vision*. London: Verso, 1986.

Sadoul, Georges. *Dictionnaire des cinéastes*. Paris: Editions du seuil, 1965.

———. *Georges Méliès*. Paris: Seghers, 1961.

Safouan, Moustapha. *La sexualité féminine dans la doctrine freudienne*. Paris: Editions du Seuil, 1976.

Said, Edward. *Beginnings*. New York: Basic Books, Inc., Publishers, 1975.

Saporta, Marc, ed. *M. Duras. l'Arc* 98, Editions LE JAS (Marseille, 1985).

Sontag, Susan. *On Photography*. New York: Farrar, Strauss, & Giroux, 1977.

Starobinski, Jean. *L'Oeil vivant*. Paris: NRF Gallimard, 1961.

Steinmetz-Schunemann, Helga. *Die Bedeutung der Zeit in den Romanen von Marguerite Duras*. Amsterdam: Rodopi, 1976.

Sternberg, Meir. *Expositional Modes and Temporal Ordering in Fiction*. Baltimore, Johns Hopkins University Press, 1978.

Sturrock, John, ed. *Structuralism and Since: From Lévi-Strauss to Derrida*. London: Oxford University Press, 1979.

Van Wert, William. "The Cinema of Marguerite Duras: Sound and Voice in a Closed Room." *Film Quarterly* 33:1 (Fall 1979): 22–29.

Vernet, Marc. *Figures de l'absence*. Cahiers du Cinéma, Collection Essais. Paris: Editions de l'Etoile, 1988.

William, Linda. "Hiroshima and Marienbad: Metaphor and Metonymy." *Screen* 17:1 (Spring 1976): 34–40.

Willis, Sharon. *Marguerite Duras: Writing on the Body*. Urbana and Chicago: University of Illinois Press, 1987.

Index